May all your trails be crooked, winding, lonesome, dangerous,
leading to the most amazing view, where something strange
and more beautiful and more full of wonder than your
deepest dreams waits for you. —EDWARD ABBEY

WESTERN NATIONAL PARKS' LODGES
COOKBOOK

Kathleen Bryant

NORTHLAND
PUBLISHING

To my mom, the very best cook of all.

—KB

www.northlandbooks.com

Composed in the United States of America
Printed in China

Edited by Claudine J. Randazzo
Designed by Sunny H. Yang

FIRST IMPRESSION 2007
ISBN 10: 0-87358-900-9
ISBN 13: 978-0-87358-900-0

11 10 09 08 07   5 4 3 2 1

Library of Congress Cataloging-in-Publication Data:

Bryant, Kathleen.
Western National Park lodges cookbook / by Kathleen Bryant.
p.cm.
ISBN 0-87358-900-9
1. Cookery. 2. Wilderness lodges—West (U.S.)—Guidebooks.
3. National parks and reserves—West (U.S.) I. Title.
TX714.B797 2007
641.5978—dc22

CONTENTS

Introduction   *1*

Yellowstone National Park   *5*
Old Faithful Inn: The First of the Great Lodges

Grand Canyon National Park   *17*
El Tovar: In Fred Harvey's Footsteps
Grand Canyon Lodge: Risen From the Ashes

Zion National Park   *37*
Zion Lodge: A Refuge for Auto Travelers

Yosemite National Park   *47*
The Ahwahnee Hotel: The Crown Jewel of the National Parks
Wawona Hotel: Victorian Romance

Death Valley National Park   *79*
Furnace Creek Inn: An Oasis in the Desert

Crater Lake National Park   *97*
Crater Lake Lodge: Rebuilding a Dream

Mount Rainier National Park   *111*
Paradise Inn: A Classic Mountain Lodge

Mount Hood National Forest   *127*
Timberline Lodge: The Pride of a Nation

Grand Teton National Park   *141*
Jackson Lake Lodge: Ushering in a New Era

Glacier National Park   *151*
Glacier Park Lodge: A Temple to Trees
Many Glacier Hotel: Where Trails Meet
Lake McDonald Lodge: Showplace on a Budget
Prince of Wales Hotel: Neighborly Hospitality

Acknowledgments   *168*
Index   *169*

Western National Parks

Mount Rainier National Park

Mount Hood National Forest

Crater Lake National Park

Yosemite National Park

Death Valley National Park

Grand Canyon National Park

Glacier National Park

Yellowstone National Park

Grand Teton National Park

Zion National Park

WASHINGTON

OREGON

NEVADA

CALIFORNIA

UTAH

ARIZONA

MONTANA

WYOMING

In any area in which the preservation of the beauty of Nature is a primary purpose, every modification of the natural landscape, whether it be construction of a road or erection of a shelter, is an intrusion. A basic objective of those who are entrusted with the development of such areas for the human uses for which they are established is, it seems to me, to hold these intrusions to a minimum and so to design them that, besides being attractive to look upon, they appear to belong to and be a part of their settings.

— STEPHEN MATHER
founding director of the National Park Service, 1916-1929

INTRODUCTION

A mere century and a half ago, the nation was struggling to define the western frontier. Its deserts and deep gashes shocked, even repelled, a country that still looked to Europe for aesthetic ideals. One 1850s traveler viewed the desert as a place with "broken wagons, dying animals, and men feeding on their carcasses, groaning in the agonies of despair and death." Even after gold was discovered in California in 1848, travelers' tales and tragedies kept all but the most adventurous, or perhaps the most desperate, in the East. The West made a fine backdrop for adventure stories, but it was not a place to go sightseeing or to raise a family.

With the completion of the intercontinental railroad in 1869, national interest in this region began to grow. Geologists and surveyors made reports, sketches, and photographs of the West's strange and wonderful sights: geysers and mud pots, fantastically shaped rock spires, ancient cliff dwellings, frozen volcanoes, salt-pan deserts.

Gradually, Americans realized the treasures in their own backyard. Europeans might have culture, but Americans had nature—vast untracked wildernesses cut by dramatic canyons and crowned by snow-peaked mountains.

By the 1880s, it was not only safe but also stylish to travel West. Outdoor enthusiasts, such as Zane Grey and Teddy Roosevelt, described a land where reality was as exciting as fiction. Publisher Charles Lummis and George Wharton James, a defrocked minister turned travel writer, preached the wonders of the Grand Canyon and other regional attractions in dozens of guidebooks. Nature writers such as John Muir and Mary Austin represented a growing conservation movement that called for setting aside tracts of scenic land.

Development of the remote western parks often depended on railroad companies, competing with each other to boost passenger traffic. To attract well-heeled travelers, "log palace" hotels began to be constructed at Yellowstone, Grand Canyon, Glacier, and other destinations, combining local ambience with comfort—even luxury. Visitors often stayed at a location for several weeks or even an entire season, and lodges became oases of civilization in remote areas.

Parks gained a champion in 1916, when Stephen Mather was appointed director of the newly formed National Park Service. Mather had a knack for finding investors for building projects and believed that appealing to the influential upper classes would ensure the future of the parks. He worked with architects to establish consistent and attractive design standards for park structures.

People visit the national parks and forests to experience nature's work. But architecture provides a framework for the human experience. A traveler's special memories might include watching a thunderstorm's dramatic approach from a balcony at Furnace Creek Inn, easing hike-sore feet in front of the crackling fireplace at Lake McDonald Lodge, or savoring an elegant meal while watching the sunset from the Mural Room restaurant at the Jackson Lake Lodge.

There is an old saying that an army travels on its stomach. Don't we all? El Tovar's executive chef, Joseph Nobile, a history buff, sees the connection between food and the human adventure. Nobile and other chefs who work at our parks' grand lodges create elegant dishes that stretch to serve hundreds of guests, in settings that present their own adventures, from ghosts in the wine cellar to ringtails in the rafters.

As Nobile says, "I can't imagine being in a city. I have the greatest job here."

YELLOWSTONE NATIONAL PARK

What a beautiful and thrilling specimen for America to preserve and hold up to the view of her refined citizens and the world in future ages! A Nation's Park, containing man and beast, in all the wild and freshness of their nature's beauty!

— GEORGE CATLIN
artist, comments on the first call for a national park in 1833

THE FIRST NATIONAL PARK in the U.S. was established by congress on March 1, 1872, with the idea of preserving a landscape most easterners could hardly imagine. Yellowstone includes ten thousand thermal features, a waterfall twice the height of Niagara Falls, several canyons, and so many big game animals that it has been called the Serengeti of the West.

Yellowstone's earliest human inhabitants were American Indians, and archaeologic evidence dates their presence to thousands of years ago. The first white man to visit Yellowstone was likely John Colter, of the Lewis and Clark Expedition, who admired the West so much he stayed after other expedition members returned home in 1806. Few others were aware of the area until 1871, when Ferdinand V. Hayden, head of the U.S. Geological Survey, assembled a survey party that included photographer William H. Jackson and artist Thomas Moran. The Hayden survey confirmed rumors of this wonderland of geology and scenery and helped inspire the establishment of the national park.

Those who wished to visit the new park had few options. They could take a Great Northern line from Bismarck for a thousand-plus miles, then travel another eight hundred miles by steamboat down the Missouri River to Fort Benton, where they would travel the final couple hundred miles by stagecoach, a journey of twelve to fourteen days. Another option was to travel from Omaha to Utah via the Union Pacific, then journey by stagecoach to Virginia City, Montana, another five hundred miles and ten days.

Wild bison still graze the open prairie inside the park.

After 1883, most visitors arrived by train to Gardiner, Montana, a more comfortable journey even though the sight of Gardiner, with one saloon for every ten residents, might have surprised those from more civilized parts. From Gardiner, they traveled by horse-drawn stages on a circular route through the park, a journey of several days, with each night spent at a different hotel, each offering a varied level of comfort.

In 1885, Yellowstone had 5,438 visitors, and a hotel was built at popular Upper Geyser Basin. Called "the Shack," it had unfinished walls that gave guests splinters, and it rattled with every step. The Shack burned down in 1894 and was replaced by an even cruder wooden building that acted as kitchen and dining room. There were tents for guestrooms. As visitation increased, so did the cry for more comfortable lodging.

OLD FAITHFUL INN
The First of the Great Lodges

The first of the great western lodges, Old Faithful Inn, was designed by Robert Reamer, who was twenty-nine years old when hired by the Northern Pacific Railway in 1902. This unknown, self-taught architect created a most unusual and impressive landmark with size and style to equal a Wild West boast.

The Old Faithful Inn is seven stories high, with a steep roof that rises up six of the seven stories. Its total length, counting later additions, is nearly seven hundred feet. The roof is wood shingles; the ground floor, hand-hewn logs; and the foundation, stone quarried nearby.

Reamer's use of local materials, his exceptional handcraft, and allusions to historic building styles set standards for all national park lodges that followed. Other railroad company executives and concessionaires no doubt began dreaming of building equally impressive lodges in "their" parks, as they witnessed the inn's popularity.

Construction began in 1903 and continued throughout the winter so that the inn would be ready to open in the spring. The lobby and its massive fireplace, which used five hundred tons of rhyolite, sheltered the work crew over a winter so cold that nails shattered on impact. The crew included trestle builders from the railroad, their skills and experience suited to making Reamer's intricately designed seven-story lobby a reality.

Reamer allegedly "sketched the plans while shakily emerging out of a monumental submersion in malt." The lobby rises eighty feet, with balconies and stairways supported by gnarled log brackets and columns—an extravagant, gigantic tree house with an interior staircase leading to a smaller tree house, the Crow's Nest, where musicians performed nightly.

Dormer windows pierce the roof letting in shafts of natural light, which angle across the beams, columns, and railings by day. Originally the bark was left on the logs, adding to the feeling of being inside a forest. (Later, when the inn closed during World War II, the logs were peeled for easier maintenance.) Reamer also designed the copper light fixtures and some of the furnishings, including a clock with a fourteen-foot face and a giant popcorn popper.

The inn is located next to its namesake, the Old Faithful geyser.

Chapman's favorite dish to prepare is Seared Elk Medallions with Madeira Sauce (page 15) served with stir-fried cabbage and pears. Game entrées are popular with guests, surprising some park service managers who thought that visitors might not want elk or bison on the menu after seeing them in the park.

Because Chapman oversees dining rooms throughout the park, he spends a week at each property when they open in the spring, then makes return visits throughout the season. In the winter, he occasionally needs to snowmobile to the lodges.

He enjoys the camaraderie of the people he works with at Yellowstone and, of course, its beauty: "If it's a nice day, and I have a two-hour drive, I might skip the company car and take my motorcycle. I see bears along the roadside, bald eagles, herds of elk, mountains, and lakes, and think to myself, 'I live here.'"

Guests entered the dining room through heavy double doors replete with hand-forged iron hinges. Scissor log trusses support the dining room roof. The half-log ceiling and log walls give the room a rustic feel. The hickory cane-backed chairs were made by the Old Hickory Furniture Company. Guests sat down to evening meals served family-style at long trestle tables.

Recapturing the dining experience of the inn's early days was one of the first duties for Yellowstone's current executive chef, Jim Chapman, when he came on board in 2003. His catering experience came in handy in planning the inn's centennial celebration, which was only a month away. Chapman researched the inn's menus from the early 1900s, drawing on them for inspiration while creating the celebration menu.

The inn's menu features many "sustainable" items, such as wild Alaskan salmon. Swordfish, sea bass, and some tunas are banned from the menu, as the Monterey Bay Aquarium deems them to be over-fished. Whenever he can, Chapman chooses local items, such as Montana Legend beef from Red Lodge, raised without hormones or antibiotics. With six hundred dinners served daily at the inn and nearly ten thousand meals a day throughout the park, menu planning and purchasing can have a significant impact. The inn and other national park lodges operated by Xanterra Parks & Resorts are working toward making menus fifty percent sustainable (featuring organic, ethical, local items) by 2015.

Opposite: The dining room's western ambience is accentuated by a log ceiling, log walls, and hickory cane-backed chairs.
Left: A signature feature of the inn, dormer windows let in shafts of light.

FORT YELLOWSTONE
Protecting the People's Park from the People

Lest the reader think that beautifully-tailored, parasol-sporting Victorian tourists behaved with more refinement and grace than do contemporary travelers, please note that the government was obliged to order the army to Yellowstone in 1886. (The original proclamation designating the nation's first park neglected to designate an operations budget or management plan.)

Soldiers fresh from the adventure of the Indian Wars had the ignominious duty of preventing tourists from chipping away at travertine terraces for souvenirs, washing their dirty laundry in hot pools, and inscribing their names onto cliff faces. Soldiers also protected tourists from themselves, as more than one curious visitor leaning in for a closer look tumbled into a hot pool or suffered steam burns from a geyser. In addition, the army dealt with poachers and bandits who preyed on wildlife and tourists.

During the summer of 1915, more than fifty thousand people visited Yellowstone. By this time, fourteen other national parks had been created. Clearly, the time was ripe for an agency solely devoted to managing the parks.

With the National Park Service's arrival at Fort Yellowstone in 1916, the army (probably with great relief) turned over bachelor officers' quarters, barracks, the chapel, and other buildings. Twenty-one of Yellowstone's soldiers transferred to the park service, becoming its first rangers.

GRILLED PEAR SALAD *with Cambozola Cheese, Toasted Walnuts, and Balsamic Glaze*

2 cups balsamic vinegar

¼ cup plus 2 cups sugar

4 cups red wine

1 cinnamon stick

5 pears, peeled, halved, and cored

1 egg white

2 tablespoons water

Pinch of cayenne

Pinch of salt

1 teaspoon sugar

1 cup walnut halves

1 pound mixed greens
(such as red oak leaf, green oak leaf, and frisée)

10 ounces Cambozola,
cut into 10 diamond shapes

Mix the vinegar and ¼ cup sugar in a small saucepan and cook to a syrupy consistency. Cool.

Mix the wine and 2 cups sugar in a medium saucepan. Add the cinnamon stick and bring to a boil. Add the pears, return to a boil, then lower heat to a simmer. Cook until the pears are tender and easily pierced by a paring knife. Allow the pears to cool in the poaching liquid.

Prepare a grill. Drain the cooled pears and cook them on the clean, oiled grill until the pears have attractive grill markings.

Preheat the oven to 350 degrees F. Mix the egg white, water, cayenne, salt, and sugar in a small bowl until thoroughly combined. Toss the walnuts in the egg mixture and then drain them in a colander. Arrange the walnuts in a single layer on a sheet pan and bake them until lightly toasted. Cool.

To serve, arrange the greens and cheese on a large platter or shallow bowl. Scatter the walnut halves on top of cheese. Fan pear halves around the cheese. Drizzle with the balsamic glaze.

Makes 10 servings

SWEET CORN BISQUE
with Linguica and Pumpkin Seeds

¼ cup butter

1 onion, diced

¼ cup flour

½ teaspoon turmeric

1 ½ quarts vegetable stock

3 pounds corn

1 potato, peeled and diced

1 pint heavy cream

Salt and white pepper

5 ounces linguica (Portuguese sausage)
cut into thin half-moons

¼ cup pumpkin seeds

Melt the butter in a soup pot and sauté the onion until translucent. Stir in flour, making a roux. Stir in the turmeric, stock, corn, potato, and cream. Bring mixture to a boil, whisking occasionally. Lower to a simmer and cook until the potatoes are very soft.

Cool soup slightly.

Purée the soup in batches using a blender. Strain. Add salt and pepper to taste. If needed, thin with more cream, stock, or milk. Gently reheat. Stir in sausage. Sprinkle with pumpkin seeds before serving.

Makes 10 servings

BREADED WILD ALASKA SALMON
with Heirloom Tomato Concassé

CONCASSÉ

1 heirloom tomato (about 6 ounces)

1 teaspoon chopped garlic

1 tablespoon extra virgin olive oil

Pinch of sugar

Salt and pepper

1 tablespoon finely shredded fresh basil

SALMON

2 fillets of wild Alaska salmon (about 6 ounces each)

Salt and white pepper

1 cup flour

2 eggs

1 tablespoon milk

2 cups panko (Japanese breadcrumbs) or dry white breadcrumbs with no crust

½ cup butter

Using a sharp knife, core the tomato and score the opposite end with an X. Place tomato in boiling water for 30 seconds, then dunk briefly in ice water so that skin will peel easily. Cut tomato in half and scoop out the seeds. Chop roughly.

Sauté the garlic in olive oil until it just begins to turn color. Add the tomato and simmer over low heat for 15 minutes. Add sugar and season to taste with salt and pepper. Just before serving stir in fresh basil.

Preheat the oven to 350 degrees F. Season salmon fillets with salt and white pepper and dredge them in flour. Beat the eggs and milk until combined. Dip the fillets in egg mixture and dredge them in panko.

Melt the butter in an ovenproof skillet. Pan-fry the breaded fillets over medium heat until golden brown. Turn the fillets and place the skillet in the oven, baking until fillets reach an internal temperature of 145 degrees.

To serve, arrange the fillets on a platter or individual plates, and pour a ribbon of Heirloom Tomato Concassé over each fillet.

Makes 2 servings

SEARED ELK MEDALLIONS
with Madeira Sauce

3 cups Madeira

Salt and pepper

2 tablespoons chilled butter, cut into small cubes

6 medallions of elk (about 2 ounces each)

¼ cup vegetable oil

Bring the Madeira to a boil, then simmer until it reaches a syrupy consistency. Season to taste with salt and pepper. Finish by whipping in the butter. Keep the sauce warm until serving, but do not boil it after adding butter.

Season the elk medallions with salt and pepper. Heat the oil in a skillet over medium-high heat. Cook the elk medallions for 1 minute on each side. To serve, lean three elk medallions against a portion of Stir-Fried Cabbage, then drizzle with Madeira sauce.

Makes 2 servings

STIR-FRIED CABBAGE

1 ½ tablespoons vegetable oil

2 cups shredded savoy cabbage

¼ cup red pepper, cut into julienne pieces

2 tablespoons peeled and grated apple

1 tablespoon minced onion

1 tablespoon sugar

1 tablespoon cider vinegar

Salt and pepper

Heat the oil in a skillet until it reaches the smoking point. Stir in the cabbage, red pepper, apple, and onion and cook over high heat, stirring constantly, for 30 seconds. Add the sugar, vinegar, salt, and pepper. Cook 30 more seconds, stirring constantly. Serve immediately.

Makes 2 servings

GRAND CANYON NATIONAL PARK

O the pretty Harvey Girl beside my chair,
A fairer maiden I shall never see.
She was winsome, she was neat, she was gloriously sweet
And she was certainly good to me.

— *Words to a popular 1907 tune*
from Ken Burn's THE WEST

GRAND CANYON IS SO VAST and rugged it seems completely beyond the human experience. Yet people have lived along its river and rim for thousands of years, leaving behind signs of their passing in rock art, stone pueblos, and pottery sherds. The Canyon's five life zones (the equivalent of traveling from Mexico to Canada) support more than two thousand species of plants, mammals, birds, reptiles, amphibians, and fish, including several endangered and threatened species.

The Canyon's cliffs, in a layered spectrum of reds, oranges, grays, and tans, record three eras of geologic time, containing rocks along the Colorado River that are two billion years old. (The Canyon itself is "only" five or six million years old, and still changing.) Venturing below the rim leads to a closer relationship with the Canyon's expanses, through hiking, backpacking, mule riding, and river rafting.

In 1903, Teddy Roosevelt urged every American to see it. On busy spring days, when the line of cars at the entry station seems endless, it appears as if everyone in the U.S. has taken his advice. But Grand Canyon National Park's mile-deep abyss and 1.2 million acres offers solitude and wilderness to those who seek it. The North Rim of the Canyon is higher, cooler, and quieter. Only one in ten of the Canyon's millions of visitors reaches its forested environs and panoramic overlooks.

Rays of sunlight enhance the colorful canyon walls as a rarely seen waterfall flows to the Canyon floor.

But even along the popular South Rim, it's possible to find a rocky perch to watch a condor soar past or gaze at cloud shadows moving across gorges and peaks. Most visitors are content to wander through historic Grand Canyon Village along the South Rim, where Rough Rider Buckey O'Neill's cabin (now part of Bright Angel Lodge) stands between Mary Colter's fabulous Lookout Studio and the gracious El Tovar hotel.

Here, the Santa Fe Railway lured visitors away from an earlier tourist center at Grandview Point by building a spur line and depot in 1902, creating architectural experiences that added to the Canyon's mystique. The Rim Trail that runs along the Canyon's edge takes visitors on a leisurely stroll past the Hopi House, the El Tovar, and the Kolb Brothers' Studio, all historic buildings that made this park a premiere destination.

EL TOVAR

In Fred Harvey's Footsteps

Between 1896 and 1920, the Santa Fe Railway built seventeen hotels, most designed in regional styles. El Tovar stands just twenty feet from Grand Canyon's South Rim, bridging the chasm between Victorian fancy and a longing to return to nature and simplicity, reflected in the popular Craftsman style that was sweeping the nation.

Though Victorian in scale, the hundred-room El Tovar was constructed with the attention to detail typified by Craftsman adherents. It was designed by Charles Whittlesey, a native of Illinois who studied with Louis Sullivan (often called "the father of modern architecture") before moving West to work for the Santa Fe Railway.

When it opened in 1905, El Tovar was an eclectic mix of Victorian ornamentation, European detailing, and rustic materials, from its rubble masonry foundation to its Queen Anne–style turret. The first floor's log slab siding has corner notching that gives the illusion of log construction. Balustrades, indoors and out, are jig sawn in chalet fashion, with a dark stain adding to the rustic ambiance. The Rendezvous Room was decorated with Arts and Crafts furniture and hunting trophies, including a mountain lion shot by western novelist Zane Grey.

The mixture could have been jarring. Instead, it radiates casual warmth and subtle elegance. Because of its remote location, the hotel was also self sustaining. El Tovar's original plans included a kitchen garden, greenhouse, dairy, and poultry barn, as well as a solarium, ladies' lounge, and billiards room. El Tovar set a standard, and its appeal to a growing number of visitors no doubt contributed to the establishment of Grand Canyon as a national monument in 1908.

Visitors praised the hotel's accommodations and the food (prepared by an Italian chef who once worked in New York and Chicago clubs) almost as extravagantly as they did the Canyon itself. One satisfied Harvey customer wrote: "It is no less astonishing than gratifying to find away out in these wastes a quail broiled to a turn and a steak more tender than a woman's love."

Built for the then unheard-of sum of two hundred fifty thousand dollars, El Tovar was refurbished during the 1980s at a price tag of nearly eleven million dollars. Today, El Tovar is owned and operated by Xanterra Parks & Resorts, whose mission includes continuing the legacy of Fred Harvey Company as well as promoting environmental standards throughout the company's properties, which include several national park lodges.

Fred Harvey built his empire on the motto "maintenance of standards, regardless of cost." His legacy is preserved throughout El Tovar, but one could speculate that the former restaurateur

The powerful stone exterior complements the vast canyon walls.

American Indian artwork and views of the Canyon enhance the dining room's elegant ambience.

might be partial to the hotel's dining room, where presidents and celebrities have enjoyed Harvey-style hospitality.

Early promotional materials likened the dining room to a traditional Norwegian hall. The dark-stained walls are decorated with painted murals depicting Arizona's native peoples. Large windows look toward the Canyon's rim. A smaller, private dining area is tucked off to one side. Legend surrounding this dark-paneled, masculine room is that it was added in 1906 for Theodore Roosevelt, who had the unfortunate habit of showing up for dinner in boots and riding clothes, a uniform not in keeping with the Harvey standards.

Sometimes, no politically correct solution presented itself. When Arizona's first governor, George W. P. Hunt, learned that El Tovar's dining room required gentlemen to wear ties, he stormed out, leading his entourage to a hotel further along the rim.

Another El Tovar tale has it that the dining room's richly stained woodwork got its sheen from nightly rubbings with coffee, a tale confirmed by history buff and executive chef Joseph Nobile, who has searched through files of historic menus and photos while investigating El Tovar's past. Nobile oversees menus for all the South Rim's lodges and coordinates with the park

service, concessionaires, and vendors to maintain Xanterra's sustainable menu program, featuring organic and local foods.

Nobile, who worked in several small family restaurants in the East before graduating from the Culinary Institute, enjoys the camaraderie of working in a national park. He finds the close-knit community like a small town despite the daily influx of thousands of visitors, many of whom eat in the lodges.

Although hungry hikers have made chili and hot chocolate the most-requested items on El Tovar's menu, Nobile most enjoys preparing the Pan-Seared Salmon Tostada (page 29). This colorful and popular dish, which has been on the menu for seven years running, plays up Arizona's Indian and Hispanic heritage.

Nobile finds the special preparations for celebrity guests one of the most interesting things about his job. "Everybody comes here eventually," he says. During his presidency, Bill Clinton visited Grand Canyon twice. Nobile, who met the former president, says that Clinton "has an aura about him that is indescribable."

Celebrity guests include Paul McCartney, who dined at El Tovar with his wife-to-be. Nobile prepared their meal and visited their table, finding them to be "most polite." As McCartney was leaving the dining room, he noticed several staff members delivering a birthday cake to one of the tables. He graciously stopped to sing happy birthday, a memorable experience for everyone in the room that night.

Though Fred Harvey, who died in 1901, never had the pleasure of dining at El Tovar himself, many hotel staff members claim to have seen him wandering about. One of Nobile's sous chefs saw an apparition in the wine cellar (a vision that didn't involve any tippling, we assume), and his description of the ghost's appearance matched a portrait of Harvey that Nobile remembers seeing during his research.

Ghosts, presidents, celebrities—and the Canyon itself, of course—make El Tovar an interesting place to work. "Grand Canyon is bigger than any one person, a very humbling place," says Nobile, who has lived and worked at the Canyon for ten years. "Since coming here, I feel humbled every day, which makes me realize it's not all about me."

Left: The hotel's expansive front porch is an excellent spot for relaxing.

FRED HARVEY
How the West was Won

The successful association forged between the Santa Fe Railway and the Fred Harvey Company changed the face of the West. Harvey, an Englishman, was appalled at the poor fare and service he found throughout train stations and depot hotels. A former restaurant owner turned freight agent, Harvey convinced the Atchison, Topeka, & Santa Fe Railroad that, given the chance, he could do better. The first Harvey House opened in 1876, and its success led to dozens of restaurants, hotels, and gift shops throughout the West.

But Fred Harvey's influence reached even further. Rough-and-tumble communities settled by prospectors, loggers, merchants, and train crews gained a touch of grace when the Santa Fe imported thousands of young women to work in Harvey lunchrooms from Topeka to Los Angeles. Harvey Girls married ranchers and other locals, and it's said that many a baby boy was christened "Fred" or "Harvey" as the wild and woolly West was tamed.

GRAND CANYON LODGE
Risen From the Ashes

Across the Canyon from El Tovar, ten miles as the raven flies, five and a half hours by vehicle, or twenty-five miles on foot, Grand Canyon Lodge welcomes visitors. However, the lodge on the North Rim has less in common with the South Rim's El Tovar than it does with lodges the Union Pacific Railway (U.P.) and its subsidiary, the Utah Parks Company, had already built in Utah.

From 1905 to 1928, the Santa Fe Railway's rustic chateau, El Tovar, offered the best of Grand Canyon accommodations on the South Rim. The Union Pacific wanted something equally elegant and noteworthy for the Canyon's North Rim, two hundred miles from the nearest U.P. line.

Not only did the U.P. want a lodge that equaled or surpassed El Tovar, Grand Canyon Lodge was to be the grand finale on the railway's U.P. Loop Tour that included Zion National Park, Bryce National Monument, and Cedar Breaks National Monument.

Gilbert Stanley Underwood's designs for lodges at Zion and Bryce and a dining pavilion at Cedar Breaks had been completed a few years before. The U.P. and its subsidiary, the Utah Parks Company, selected Underwood again as architect for Grand Canyon Lodge. Underwood had just completed the fabulous Ahwahnee Hotel in Yosemite, and the lodge on the North Rim promised to be as successful.

Design began in 1927, with construction later that year. The building site was on the very edge of Bright Angel Point. Limestone was quarried from a site two miles away. Timber came from the Kaibab Forest, about ten miles north, and was milled on site. Because the mill required water and power, a hydroelectric plant was built on the Colorado River, more than three thousand feet below the construction site.

Grand Canyon Lodge shared a similarity with the other U.P. Loop lodges, and yet it had an air of refinement that structures at Zion, Bryce, and Cedar Breaks did not, possibly because of Underwood's recent experience designing the elegant Ahwahnee. At the same time, Grand Canyon Lodge was much more rustic than The Ahwahnee, with strong horizontal lines that echoed the layering of the Canyon itself.

Underwood banked the stonework foundation into the rim, and parts of the building looked like rocky outcroppings rising

Opposite: The dining room's expansive windows offer limitless views of the Canyon.
Below: The stone patio is a perfect place to watch the sunset before or after an excellent meal.

The lodge as it is today, rebuilt after the 1932 fire, without the original observation tower.

up out of the Canyon's cliffs, a style used across the Canyon by Mary Colter for Lookout Studio. Underwood incorporated the rim and its vistas into his design, adding multiple levels of open terraces that overlooked the Canyon.

As at the other U.P. lodges, Grand Canyon Lodge guest rooms were not part of the main lodge. Visitors stayed in satellite cabins, ranging from beautifully equipped deluxe cabins with their own porches to more modest standard cabins. When the Lodge opened in 1928, there were twenty deluxe cabins northeast of the lodge and one hundred standard cabins, smaller and closer together, to the southwest. Even the more modest standard cabins

were situated according to the forested, hilly topography of the site rather than in straight rows.

The Union Pacific altered Underwood's design in one key respect. His original plan called for a structural core of concrete and steel. Perhaps in an effort to save money, company officials made the fateful decision to use a timber frame instead.

On June 1, 1928, the lodge and cabins opened their doors, with room for up to two hundred fifty guests. For four years the Grand Canyon Lodge was the highlight of the U.P. Loop. Then, early on the morning of September 1, 1932, sparks from a fire-place in the main lodge started what was the largest structural fire

throughout large public spaces, and painted and carved Indian symbols contribute to the building's sense of style and place. Exposed roof trusses (this time steel covered by logs) soar above the lodge's public areas including the lobby, the recreation room, and the dining room, which is located through the lobby at the back of the hotel.

Here visitors can enjoy views while dining on Pasta Sublime (page 32), named after a popular North Rim overlook, or Kaibab Chicken, from the Paiute word for "mountain lying down." Gazing at the ever-shifting yet eternal Canyon, you might find yourself acknowledging Underwood's skill at inviting people to form a deeper appreciation of the park's natural environment.

Left: An early photo of the lodge before the devastating fire in 1932.

in the history of Grand Canyon National Park. The lodge and two deluxe cabins were completely destroyed, save for the stone foundation and chimneys.

In the aftermath, Horace Albright, the director of the National Park Service at the time, wrote to Union Pacific officials: "It seemed a crime that this wonderful lodge had to be destroyed … I hope you will find it possible to rebuild the lodge at once, as your operation at the Grand Canyon was the outstanding tourist accommodation of the entire national park system."

In 1936, a new lodge did open on the original site, but one popular feature, the observation tower, was missing. Other changes included a steeper roof pitch helpful for shedding North Rim snows. This was an alteration that shifted the flavor of Underwood's original design from a low-roofed Craftsman or Spanish Revival style to a design that is more purely rustic.

The reconstruction, while not as grand than the original Grand Canyon Lodge, is still impressive. The U-shaped roofline of the main lodge varies with broken pitches and dormers. On the lodge's south side, large windows overlook the Canyon, as do the open terraces. The east terrace has a huge fireplace—large enough to stand in.

Railroad engineers supervised the reconstruction, yet Underwood's influence is evident in the lodge's sense of scale and drama. Massive wrought-iron chandeliers and sconces hang

THE U.P. LOOP
Partnering with the Parks

The scenery of the national parks drew more visitors when comfortable and attractive lodging awaited at journey's end. The Santa Fe, Canadian Pacific, and Great Northern railroads had already built resort hotels and spurs near their main lines, and the Union Pacific was anxious to compete by erecting its own "log palaces."

During the 1920s, the Union Pacific constructed a spur line to Cedar City. Railroad officials realized they could move freight out of Cedar City on the spur line and increase revenues with passenger traffic on the main line. Recognizing the potential of the southern Utah–Arizona region, they created a subsidiary, the Utah Parks Company.

The Utah Parks Company invested millions to improve areas in and around the parks, advertising in popular magazines and launching ten-day rail, bus, and limousine tours encompassing the North Rim of the Grand Canyon, Bryce Canyon National Park, Cedar Breaks National Monument, and Zion Canyon. The journey came to be known as the "U.P. Loop."

Gilbert Stanley Underwood designed buildings at all four parks on the U.P. Loop. Grand Canyon Lodge and its associated structures are the most complete development of the era's railroad-built rustic architecture that remain standing today.

BLACK BEAN SOUP

EL TOVAR

1 ½ pounds (about 3 cups) dried black beans

4 ounces bacon fat

2 onions, diced

2 cloves garlic, minced

1 gallon chicken stock

2 smoked ham hocks

¾ cup sherry

2 tablespoons red wine vinegar

2 tablespoons Tabasco

1 tablespoon chili powder

½ tablespoon ground cumin

1 teaspoon salt

¼ teaspoon pepper

1 (10-ounce) package corn tortillas

Lime Sour Cream

1 bunch scallions, chopped at a diagonal

Cover the beans with water and soak them for several hours or overnight. Drain the beans, discarding liquid. Heat the bacon fat in a heavy-bottomed pot. Add the onions and sauté until translucent. Add the minced garlic and sauté 2 more minutes, stirring constantly. Add the chicken stock and bring mixture to a simmer. Add the ham hocks and beans. Return to a simmer and cook until the beans are tender.

Remove the ham hocks and allow them to cool. Trim away fat and dice the meat. Return the diced ham hocks to the soup. Add sherry, red wine vinegar, Tabasco, chili powder, cumin, salt, and pepper. Simmer for 20 minutes.

In the meantime, preheat oven to 325 degrees F. Cut the tortillas into strips and bake them until crisp. Purée the soup in a blender, two cups at a time. Ladle soup into bowls and garnish with Lime Sour Cream (page 31), chopped scallions, and tortilla strips before serving.

Makes 10 to 16 servings

BLUE CORN TAMALES

EL TOVAR

1 pound (8-ounce package) cornhusks

½ pound blue cornmeal

1 pound masa harina

1 tablespoon ground cumin

¼ teaspoon baking powder

1 tablespoon chili powder

1 teaspoon salt

1 ½ cups vegetable shortening

1 quart cold water

3 ripe avocados

Juice of 2 limes

2 cloves garlic, minced

½ red onion, finely diced

½ red bell pepper, diced

½ jalapeño, seeded and minced

1 medium tomato, diced

2 tablespoons chopped fresh cilantro

1 (15-ounce) can black beans, drained and rinsed

Salt and pepper

Soak the cornhusks in warm water until they soften. In the meantime, prepare the masa and filling.

Combine the cornmeal, masa harina, cumin, chili powder, baking powder, and salt and blend together on low speed. Mix in the shortening a spoonful at a time, until the mixture clumps into little balls. Slowly add the cold water, mixing until the masa holds together. You may not need all the water. Cover the masa and set it aside at room temperature.

Mash the avocados with lime juice. Stir in the garlic, onion, bell pepper, jalapeño, tomato, cilantro, and beans. Season to taste with salt and pepper. If you are not using the guacamole filling immediately, cover it with plastic wrap, placing the wrap directly on the filling to prevent it from turning brown, and refrigerate it.

Drain the softened cornhusks. Assemble the tamales one at a time. Spread 3 tablespoons of masa on a cornhusk. Place 2 tablespoons of filling in the center of the masa, leaving an inch of masa around the edges of the filling. Fold the left and right sides of the cornhusk to the center, and then pull the tail end to the center. Repeat until all the tamales are rolled.

Arrange the tamales in a steamer basket and place it over boiling water. Cover and steam for 20 minutes. (A bamboo steamer is perfect for this.)

Serve the tamales with Fire-Roasted Corn Salsa (page 30).

Makes 12 tamales

PAN-SEARED SALMON TOSTADAS

EL TOVAR

½ cup canola oil

4 (6-inch) blue corn tortillas

4 (6-inch) red corn tortillas

4 salmon fillets, about 6 ounces each

6 ounces spring or mesclun lettuce mix

Chile-Olive Oil

Chile-Lime Rice

Fire-Roasted Corn Salsa

Lime Sour Cream

Preheat the oven to 350 degrees F. Bake the blue and red tortillas until crisp. Set aside.

Heat the oil in a skillet. Sear salmon fillets in hot oil, about 4 minutes per side for medium-rare. Set aside and keep warm.

Toss the lettuce mix with Chile-Olive Oil (page 31), just enough to coat the greens lightly.

To serve, place a portion of Chile-Lime Rice (page 31) on each plate at 12 o'clock. Arrange one red and one blue tortilla on each plate at 4 and 8 o'clock. Divide the dressed greens and place on top of the tortillas on each plate. Place a salmon fillet on top of the greens. Top each fillet with a spoonful of Fire-Roasted Corn Salsa (page 30). Use a squeeze bottle to garnish with Lime Sour Cream (page 31).

Makes 4 servings

FIRE-ROASTED CORN SALSA

EL TOVAR

3 ears fresh sweet corn

Canola oil

1 tomato, chopped

¼ green bell pepper, finely chopped

¼ red bell pepper, finely chopped

½ jalapeño, seeded and minced

¼ red onion, finely chopped

1 tablespoon chopped cilantro

½ cup V-8 juice

⅛ teaspoon salt

⅛ teaspoon ground black pepper

Prepare a grill. Generously coat each ear of corn with the oil before grilling. Cool before cutting the kernels from each cob with a sharp knife.

Combine the corn, tomato, red and green bell pepper, jalapeño, onion, cilantro, V-8 juice, salt, and pepper. Mix thoroughly. Cover and set salsa aside at room temperature for an hour before serving to allow flavors to blend.

Makes about 2 cups

CHILE OLIVE OIL EL TOVAR

1 cup olive oil

1 tablespoon ancho chile paste

1 teaspoon Tabasco

Combine olive oil, chile paste, and Tabasco, mixing well.
Pour mixture into a plastic bottle with a squirt top.
Keep at room temperature. Shake well before using.

Makes 4 servings

CHILE-LIME RICE EL TOVAR

½ tablespoon vegetable oil

½ medium yellow onion, finely chopped

½ teaspoon minced garlic

2 tablespoons tomato paste

Juice of 2 limes

3 cups cooked white rice, room temperature

½ tablespoon chili powder

1 teaspoon finely chopped cilantro

Salt and pepper

Heat the oil over medium-high heat. Add the onion and sauté until translucent. Add the minced garlic and sauté, stirring, until slightly browned. Stir in tomato paste and cook until mixture caramelizes and turns slightly brown. Deglaze the pan with the lime juice.

Add the rice and stir in chili powder and chopped cilantro. Continue stirring until the rice is heated through. Season to taste with salt and pepper.

Makes 4 servings

LIME SOUR CREAM EL TOVAR

1 (8-ounce) carton sour cream

2 tablespoons lime juice

Whisk together the sour cream and lime juice until combined.
Pour mixture into a plastic bottle with a squirt top.
Keep refrigerated until ready to use.

Makes 1 cup

PASTA SUBLIME

GRAND CANYON LODGE

4 ounces sun-dried tomatoes

¼ cup olive oil

6 cloves garlic, minced

2 medium shallots, minced

3 tablespoons white wine

3 ounces fresh basil, shredded

Salt and pepper

¾ pound linguini

Cover the sun-dried tomatoes with cold water and soak for 4 hours to rehydrate. Drain and discard any unabsorbed water before using them.

Heat the olive oil in a large skillet and sauté the garlic and shallots. Add the wine and cook until reduced by half. Add the sun-dried tomatoes and fresh basil. Season to taste with salt and pepper.

Prepare linguini according to package directions. Add drained pasta to the skillet and toss to ensure even coverage. Serve in pasta bowls or on plates.

Makes 2 servings

SMOKED SALMON SPINACH SALAD

GRAND CANYON LODGE

¾ pound smoked salmon

3 cups spring mix

3 cups roughly chopped romaine lettuce

2 thin slices red onion, separated into rings

30 grape tomatoes

½ cup shredded carrots

Miso Vinaigrette

Break up salmon into bite-size pieces. Place with greens, onion, tomatoes, and carrots in a large mixing bowl. Toss with Miso Vinaigrette just before serving.

Makes 4 servings

MISO VINAIGRETTE   GRAND CANYON LODGE

⅔ cup vegetable oil

¼ cup rice wine vinegar

2 tablespoons honey

2 cloves garlic, minced

⅛ teaspoon white pepper

½ teaspoon salt

1 teaspoon Dijon mustard

2 tablespoons miso

½ teaspoon dried crushed basil

Combine all ingredients in a jar with a tight-fitting lid. Cover and shake well. Serve immediately, or store in the refrigerator for up to three days.

Makes about 1 cup

NEW YORK STRIP STEAKS
with Béarnaise Sauce

GRAND CANYON LODGE

¼ cup red wine vinegar

Juice of 1 lemon

2 medium shallots, minced

1 tablespoon dried tarragon

6 egg yolks

6 tablespoons clarified butter, melted

Dash of Tabasco

4 New York strip steaks, about 10 ounces each

2 tablespoons olive oil

Salt and pepper

Cook the vinegar, lemon juice, shallots, and tarragon in a small saucepan until reduced by three-quarters. Cool.

Place the egg yolks in a skillet and whisk them constantly while cooking over medium heat, adding the butter gradually to ensure proper emulsification. Whisk in the cooled vinegar reduction. Set aside in a warm place.

Preheat a grill. Rub the steaks with a light coating of olive oil and season with salt and pepper. Cook to desired doneness. To serve, arrange the steaks on a plate and cover each with ¼ cup of sauce.

Makes 4 servings

KAIBAB CHICKEN

GRAND CANYON LODGE

3 tablespoons olive oil

2 boneless chicken breasts

¼ cup flour

½ cup white wine

4 ounces baby spinach

4 ounces sun-dried tomatoes

¾ cup heavy cream

2 tablespoons Dijon mustard

Heat the oil in a large sauté pan. Dredge the chicken breasts in flour and sauté until done on one side. Turn them over to cook on the other side. Deglaze the pan with white wine and cook until the liquid is reduced by half.

Stir in the heavy cream. Add the spinach and sun-dried tomatoes. Cook for 3 minutes, or until thick and bubbly. Stir in mustard, mixing evenly.

Remove the chicken breasts with tongs and arrange on a serving platter or individual plates. Pour sauce over the top before serving.

Makes 2 servings

ZION NATIONAL PARK

Never before has such a naked mountain of rock entered our minds. Without a shred of disguise its transcendent form rises pre-eminent. There is almost nothing to compare to it. Niagara has the beauty of energy; the Grand Canyon of immensity; the Yellowstone of singularity; the Yosemite of altitude; the ocean of power; this Great Temple of eternity.

— FREDERICK S. DELLENBAUGH
1903, writing about Zion's Great Temple rock formation

ION IS AN ANCIENT Hebrew word referring to a place of peace and refuge. Zion National Park in southwestern Utah protects 229 square miles of some of the most scenic canyon country in the United States, a refuge for plants, wildlife, and the human spirit. The park's diverse landscapes include steep-sided canyons and sculptured rock formations with names such as the Great White Throne, the Court of the Patriarchs, and the Sentinel.

Zion's landscape has long offered shelter and refuge to humans. Paleo-Indians followed game through the canyons. The ancestral Puebloans left behind cliff houses and rock art. Trappers and traders passed through while traveling the Old Spanish Trail. During the 1860s, Mormons established several nearby communities, their cotton crops inspiring the nickname "Utah's Dixie."

An 1872 survey party led by explorer John Wesley Powell made the first area maps. Powell named it Mukuntuweap, a Paiute word meaning "straight river." The Mormons preferred Zion. Though refuge it was, making a living was tough. Settlers struggled to overcome riverside flooding, droughts, and poor soil. When cotton crops didn't generate enough money, locals hoped opening the canyon to tourism would.

In July 1909, President William Howard Taft declared more than fifteen thousand acres Mukuntuweap National Monument. The remote location and rough roads made travel difficult, and during its early years, the monument had fewer than a thousand visitors.

For thousands of years water flowing over Zion's rocks has transformed the landscape, creating unique formations.

Utah began constructing a highway system to improve access to the southern region, negotiating with the Union Pacific Railroad to develop tourism facilities in the area. On November 19, 1919, Mukuntuweap, now called Zion, became the nineteenth national park. However, even with national park status, few visitors made the rugged journey to Zion.

One visitor who did brave the rough roads again and again, was Stephen Mather, director of the National Park Service. Mather visited Zion at least once a year from 1919 to 1929, often bringing influential traveling companions. It was during one of his annual trips that the idea of a circle tour came up.

With Mather's influence, a mile-long tunnel was built through the sandstone cliffs of Zion Canyon. The Zion/Mt. Carmel Tunnel and highway, completed in 1930, took hours off the time needed to tour the Grand Circle that encompassed Bryce, Cedar Breaks, Zion, and the North Rim of the Grand Canyon. The highway encouraged travel by car, and the number of visitors to Zion jumped from fewer than four thousand people in 1920 to more than fifty-five thousand in 1930.

ZION LODGE

A Refuge for Auto Travelers

With visitation increasing, Zion needed a lodge. A Union Pacific architect drew the first plans, but Stephen Mather and Daniel Hull, a senior NPS landscape engineer, rejected the design. Hull suggested a former classmate, Gilbert Stanley Underwood, for the job.

In May 1923, Underwood was hired and sent to survey both Zion and Bryce canyons. For Zion, Underwood proposed a hotel structure with a central lobby and wings. Stephen Mather rejected this design, too, hoping for a structure that would blend with the environment and meet the needs of the growing number of automobile travelers, a new factor in park management.

Underwood's answer was a smaller lodge surrounded by cabins, a design hallmark he used also at Bryce and the North Rim of the Grand Canyon. To help the lodge blend with its surroundings, he specified native materials, sandstone quarried nearby and timber cut above the canyon rim and delivered to the site on cables.

The lodge's massive pillars of sandstone offered an impressive entry and supported a second-story balcony. The resulting strong vertical lines echoed the backdrop of sandstone cliffs. Full-length, multi-paned windows allowed natural light to flow into the building.

Construction commenced in 1924, with additional cottages and wings added over the next five years. Underwood continued to update and design various park service buildings at Zion until 1934. All were compatible with the rustic style envisioned by Mather, but only a few have stood the test of time.

Built to last throughout the twenty-year concessionaire agreement, the structures needed frequent remodeling. In January 1966, a work crew using blowtorches to help soften and remove some old vinyl flooring started a fire that began to burn furiously. A U.P. crew fought the flames until a park service team arrived with a pumper truck. But by day's end, the main lodge was reduced to its stone fireplace and pillars.

Fortunately, the fifteen deluxe guest cabins were far enough from the lodge to be spared. Underwood had designed the cabins with two or four rooms that could be made into suites. Each cabin

Zion Lodge is almost camouflaged as it nestles at the base of the canyon wall.

featured stone fireplaces, rocking chairs, and wicker writing desks. Rough-dressed stone foundations and ashlar-patterned chimneys reflected the design of the main lodge. Today, these fifteen cabins, along with a few support buildings and the Zion Nature Center, stand as the only examples of Underwood's architectural ingenuity at Zion National Park.

The U.P. decided to raze and rebuild the lodge, and the new building opened just 108 days after the fire. But it was a new era, with tighter budgets and different priorities, and the charm of Underwood's original design was lost. In 1992, ambitious plans were launched to restore some of the features of the original lodge, including the sandstone entry columns. The Red Rock Grill dining room was restored to a 1930s-era rustic style—informal, yet gracious. The second-floor dining room offers spectacular views of the canyon setting.

Recently, the remodeling project reached the kitchen. For much of one winter, food and beverage director Ed Treanor and his staff continued to serve diners while the kitchen was being renovated, turning out elegant meals from the lodge's snack bar.

Treanor owned three or four restaurants before going to culinary school. He and his wife have been at Zion for two years, after working at Grand Teton, Denali, and Yosemite.

Treanor finds it impossible to get bored at Zion because each day brings something different. One summer, for example, a thunderstorm knocked out the lodge's electricity, and his staff scrambled to prepare box lunches for everyone. At Zion, local wildlife wanders right up to the lodge's back door, where it's possible to sit and watch deer or wild turkeys.

Sometimes the wildlife even comes *through* the back door. One morning, a ringtail snatched a muffin from the breakfast buffet before bounding away. On another occasion, a skunk wandered into the kitchen. Someone locked the uninvited guest inside the cold food area until the park service could come and capture it, but the skunk escaped and headed across the dining room, with the staff right behind him

"I got a couple feet from him and herded him to the patio door," Treanor explained, a task beyond the call of duty for a chef anywhere else but all in a day's work at Zion National Park.

Opposite: The Red Rock Grill dining room reflects the 1930s era of its origination.

Left: The front desk is banked with native stone, reminding visitors of the mesmerizing rocks that beckon just out the lodge's front door.

GILBERT STANLEY UNDERWOOD
The Creator of "Parkitecture"

Architect Gilbert Stanley Underwood (a graduate of Yale and Harvard) opened an office in Los Angeles in 1923, a time when Craftsman, Beaux Arts, and Spanish Revival styles popped up in Pasadena and other fashionable neighborhoods. He carried the Craftsman aesthetic of honest materials and handcrafted details to his next assignments, designing buildings for the fledgling National Park Service.

Underwood's designs maintained a hand-built character even in larger scale. He incorporated pioneer and American Indian themes, creating buildings from local materials so that they not only blended with the landscape but also reflected regional history and culture. This style, which came to be known as "parkitecture," was exactly what parks director Stephen Mather had envisioned.

Underwood designed lodges at all of the parks on the U.P. Loop: Cedar Breaks, Zion, Bryce Canyon, and the North Rim of Grand Canyon. He also designed the fabulous Ahwahnee Hotel in Yosemite, Sun Valley Lodge in Idaho, and made the preliminary designs for Timberline Lodge in Oregon.

Underwood established design aesthetics for the parks during the 1920s, guided WPA projects throughout the 1930s, and inspired projects of the park service's Mission 66 Program—a truly remarkable career.

NAVAJO EGGPLANT

1 small to medium eggplant

Salt

10 tomatillos

½ cup heavy cream

Salt and pepper

¾ cup flour for dredging

3 eggs, beaten

½ cup panko (Japanese breadcrumbs)

¼ cup oil

Kosher salt

Freshly ground white pepper

½ cup shredded Jack cheese

1 cup Pico de Gallo

1 cup fresh baby spinach leaves

4 teaspoons finely chopped fresh cilantro for garnish

Slice the eggplant into rounds ¼- to ⅜-inch thick, making at least 12 rounds. Sprinkle the eggplant with salt and set aside for 25 to 30 minutes to draw moisture from the eggplant.

In the meantime, prepare a tomatillo cream sauce. Preheat the oven broiler. Remove the husks and cores from the tomatillos and slice each in half. Place halves on a lightly oiled sheet pan and place in the oven to broil. Watch closely, cooking until the tomatillos are slightly browned and skins are blistered. Cool. Place tomatillos and cream in a blender and blend until smooth. Season to taste with salt and pepper and set aside.

Blot the eggplant with paper towels. Season the flour with salt and pepper. Arrange three shallow bowls or plates, one with seasoned flour, one with beaten eggs, and one with breadcrumbs and dredge each eggplant round in that order. Heat the oil in a skillet and arrange eggplant rounds in a single layer. Turn the eggplant to brown both sides and cook until done. Set aside and keep warm.

Preheat the oven to 350 degrees F. Place four eggplant rounds on a lightly oiled sheet pan. Cover with a layer of tomatillo cream sauce. Continue layering eggplant rounds and cream sauce, making four stacks. Sprinkle Jack cheese over the top of the last layer of cream sauce. Bake until the cheese melts.

Warm the Pico de Gallo (page 45). Divide spinach leaves between four plates. Place an eggplant stack on the center of the spinach leaves on each plate. Top with Pico de Gallo and freshly chopped cilantro.

Makes 4 servings

PRICKLY PEAR–SMOKED TROUT SALAD

3 cups organic baby spinach

3 cups organic chopped romaine lettuce

1 pound smoked trout, flaked

1 cup Prickly Pear Vinaigrette

1 small red onion, sliced and separated into rings

½ pound organic grape tomatoes

2 tablespoons sliced almonds, toasted

Place the greens and flaked trout in a non-reactive bowl. Add Prickly Pear Vinaigrette and toss to coat completely. Top with grape tomatoes, onion rings, and almonds.

Makes 4 servings

PRICKLY PEAR VINAIGRETTE

1 (8-ounce) bottle prickly pear syrup

2 tablespoons red wine vinegar

2 tablespoons pasteurized liquid egg

¼ cup light vegetable oil (safflower or canola)

Kosher salt

White pepper

Combine the prickly pear syrup, red wine vinegar, and liquid egg in a blender. Blend, adding the vegetable oil slowly. Season to taste with salt and pepper and blend again. Refrigerate until serving.

Makes 2 cups

SANTA FE STEAK

2 cups canola or other oil for deep-frying

1 medium yellow onion

2 tablespoons Tabasco

1 cup flour

Kosher salt

White pepper

1 tablespoon finely chopped parsley

4 flatiron or rib-eye steaks, 8 to 10 ounces each

1 cup Pico de Gallo

1 cup crumbled blue cheese

Preheat the oil in a deep skillet or fryer. To make onion straws, slice the onion very thinly with a sharp knife or mandoline. Separate the onion slices into rings and place them in a mixing bowl. Coat them lightly with Tabasco. In another bowl, season the flour with salt and pepper and stir in parsley. Toss the onion straws with seasoned flour until coated. Deep-fry the onion straws and set them aside on paper towels to cool.

Prepare grill and preheat oven to 350 degrees F. Grill steaks to desired doneness. Place the steaks on a sheet pan, topping each with a portion of Pico de Gallo, onion straws, and crumbled blue cheese. Bake until the cheese starts to melt. Serve immediately.

Makes 4 servings

PICO DE GALLO

1 ½ cups finely diced tomatoes

½ cup finely diced yellow onion

¼ cup finely chopped fresh cilantro

2 tablespoons lime juice

Kosher salt

Finely ground white pepper

Combine the tomatoes, onion, cilantro, and lime juice in a non-reactive mixing bowl. Season to taste with salt and pepper. Cover and refrigerate until flavors blend. Pico de Gallo can be prepared a day in advance.

Makes 2 cups

YOSEMITE NATIONAL PARK

*Yosemite Valley, to me, is always a sunrise, a glitter of green
and golden wonder in a vast edifice of stone and space.*

— ANSEL ADAMS

THOUGH YELLOWSTONE WAS the first national park designated by congress, Yosemite can make a claim to being first by intention. In June 1864, President Abraham Lincoln signed the Yosemite Grant, legislation setting aside Yosemite Valley and the Mariposa Grove as parkland to protect the natural scenery. The intent was to preserve the area for the entire nation; however, guardianship was granted to the state of California.

The Yosemite Grant included the granite monuments, meadows, waterfalls, and rivers of the scenic Yosemite Valley as well as the giant sequoias of the Mariposa Grove south of the Valley. One of the earliest visitors was a young man named John Muir, who spent the summer of 1869 tramping among the Valley's granite monuments with a herd of sheep. He later joined preservationists lobbying for Yosemite's return to federal management, believing that state control was inadequate to deal with the increasing numbers of tourists.

Until the late 1870s, visitors who wanted to see Yosemite's geologic wonders took stagecoaches most of the way, then made the final descent into the Valley on horseback. Most were wealthy easterners and Europeans who, according to Muir, climbed onto their horses like "overgrown frogs." Yosemite Valley was soon dotted with tent camps, stables, stores, hotels, and saloons—what Muir referred to as valley-bottom "harmless scum."

The view from Olmstead Point on the east side of the park offers a very different view of Half Dome and the effects of glaciers that passed by thousands of years ago.

The area was granted national park status on October 1, 1906, in a bill signed by President Theodore Roosevelt. The National Park Service was formed in 1916, and not long afterward Director Stephen Mather wrote that Americans had the right to visit parks "in as great luxury as each can afford."

And so they did. On the day the unpaved All-Year Highway was completed in 1926, local mechanics repaired more than three hundred flat tires. In January 1927, visitation was almost seven hundred times higher than in January 1926, and the park hadn't anticipated the avalanche of unruly campers. The age of the automobile had begun...

THE AHWAHNEE HOTEL
The Crown Jewel of the National Parks

On hearing that Lady Astoria refused to stay in Yosemite Valley because of the crude lodgings available at that time, National Park Service director Stephen Mather began to envision a luxury hotel for the park. In 1925 he persuaded competing local businesses to consolidate into the Yosemite Park and Curry Company (YP&CC), sweetening the deal with two hundred thousand dollars of his own personal fortune.

One of the first priorities for YP&CC was a new year-round hotel. As Mather insisted, "Scenery is a hollow enjoyment to a tourist who sets out in the morning after an indigestible breakfast and fitful sleep on an impossible bed."

Gilbert Stanley Underwood, thirty-five years old and still basking in the success of his lodge designs for Zion and Bryce national parks, began work on The Ahwahnee in 1925. The hotel was to be set like a jewel in a grassy meadow with the Royal Arches as a backdrop, surrounded by views of Half Dome, Glacier Point, and Yosemite Falls.

Underwood continued his approach of harmonizing park structures with nature, this time incorporating modern touches. The one hundred fifty thousand-square-foot hotel was built with a steel frame. The roof is slate, with wood being used only for exterior balconies and the dining room's ceiling framing. The Ahwahnee's "redwood" siding is actually concrete poured in molds formed to look like timber, then stained.

Though the central core of The Ahwahnee is six stories tall, multiple hip and gable roofs, along with balconies, terraces, chimneys, and floor-to-ceiling windows break up the building's massing. Varying textures and heights echo the rough cliff faces surrounding the hotel.

One thousand tons of steel, five thousand tons of stone, and thirty thousand board feet of timber arrived at the site via rough roads. Two hundred workers used horses to move boulders into place. Plans were altered on the spot as Underwood, YP&CC, the contractor, park service, and other federal and state agencies wrangled over the design and costs. By the time The Ahwahnee opened—six months later than projected—its price tag had risen to more than double the original estimate.

The beautiful grounds that surround the hotel combined with breathtaking views make for one of the most picturesque settings to be found.

Though the process wasn't necessarily a harmonious one, the result pleased Mather, who wrote the press release announcing the hotel's opening and giving the public his view of the grand hotel: "The Ahwahnee is designed quite frankly for people who know the delights of luxurious living, and to whom the artistic and material comforts of their environment is important."

These comforts included an automobile entrance, private bathrooms, a ballroom, a cathedral-like dining room, and gardens designed by Frederick Law Olmstead, Jr. Here, a cosmopolitan crowd of Hollywood stars, politicians, and diplomats could enjoy the outdoors by day and dress for dinner in the evening.

But not everyone was pleased with the new hotel. A young photographer in love with Yosemite's landscape objected to The Ahwahnee's grandeur. "The architect had tried to compete with the environment. He lost." Photographer Ansel Adams eventually softened toward The Ahwahnee. He even wrote some of the hotel's promotional materials and often gave impromptu recitals on the Great Lounge's Steinway grand piano. The concerts drew such large crowds that hotel management began offering afternoon tea in the lounge, now a tradition.

Though designed and lavishly furnished with well-heeled visitors in mind, The Ahwahnee also boasts stunning public spaces that every park visitor can admire. The twenty-four-foot high ceiling of the Great Lounge is held by exposed girders and beams painted with Indian designs. The lounge's cut sandstone fireplaces, original seventeenth-century English tables, Gothic chandeliers, stained glass windows, and museum-quality Middle Eastern rugs give the room a medieval atmosphere, which is echoed throughout the hotel.

The hotel's three wings pivot around the central Elevator Lobby, which blends Indian, English Tudor, and Art Deco influences. Other public rooms include the Main Lobby, Solarium, and Mural Room, with a wall-length painting of local flora and fauna by Robert Boardman Howard that is reminiscent of medieval tapestries.

Today, some ninety thousand guests stay at The Ahwahnee each year. Past visitors have included presidents and movie stars: Herbert Hoover, the Churchills, Dwight Eisenhower, John F. Kennedy, Ronald Reagan, Charlie Chaplin, Greta Garbo, Desi Arnez and Lucille Ball, Judy Garland, Shirley Temple, Jack Benny, Red Skelton, Will Rogers, and Walt Disney.

During World War II, The Ahwahnee underwent major changes when it became a convalescent hospital for the U.S. Navy. In 1983, the sixth floor was remodeled for Queen Elizabeth and Prince Philip's visit. In 1993, Delaware North Companies took over the hotel's management, agreeing to donate the hotel and other Yosemite buildings to the government over a period of time.

Part-time valley resident Ansel Adams, who died in 1984, became one of The Ahwahnee's most beloved guests. He often breakfasted in the hotel's magnificent dining room, the only room in the entire building that isn't fireproof. The 6,630-square-foot dining room offers the traditional lodge feel of other national park hotels, with a thirty-four-foot high ceiling supported by sugar pine roof trusses, an Underwood specialty, disguising an underlying steel frame and concrete piers painted to look like logs. Stone walls alternate with floor-to-ceiling windows that frame dramatic views of Yosemite Falls and the Valley's towering granite cliffs.

Adams was a driving force behind another of The Ahwahnee's most treasured traditions, the Bracebridge Dinner. Every holiday season since December 1927, the dining room has been transformed into a seventeenth-century manor hall inspired by scenes from Washington Irving's *Sketch Book* describing Christmas at Bracebridge Hall.

The Bracebridge Dinner is a four-hour extravaganza of food, costume, and music featuring more than a hundred actors portraying Squire Bracebridge and his family, their servants, the Lord of Misrule, minstrels, and other performers. Over the years, Adams performed various stage roles and created the pageant's script, which is used to this day.

The highlight is the seven-course meal prepared by The Ahwahnee's culinary staff, featuring sumptuous dishes. The menu, different each year, is planned months in advance. Past menus have included such delights as Pickled Quail Eggs, Pheasant Dumplings,

Underwood designed the hotel to look as though it was built with heavy logs; however, those logs are actually fireproof concrete piers painted to look like wood.

and Wild Mushroom Ragout, which are served amidst a raucous and celebratory performance.

Tickets often sell out long in advance, even though the event has expanded from one evening to several. At a recent Bracebridge Dinner, executive chef Percy Whatley noticed an uninvited guest: a ringtail cat, perched on a wall sconce hidden in the shadowy ceiling trusses, watched the evening's spectacle as the dining staff watched him.

The Ahwahnee kitchen is an enormous sixty-five hundred square feet, with its own pastry and bakeshop and a staff of more than fifty. The kitchen serves an average of a thousand meals a day, as well as creating special events such as the Bracebridge Dinner or the annual Vintners' Holiday.

Chef Whatley first began working in Yosemite in 1989 as a pizza cook in a Curry Village burger stand. Even after working his way up the ladder in several Yosemite restaurants, Whatley started at the bottom again when he joined The Ahwahnee staff, working as a salad maker. While at The Ahwahnee he "caught the fine food bug" and decided to attend the Culinary Institute in New York.

Whatley worked at a resort in Lake Tahoe, then at the Wawona Hotel, before rejoining The Ahwahnee in 2003. One of his favorite tasks has been creating the Vintners' Holiday dinners, gala meals with wine pairings. "It really challenges me from a menu-writing perspective," he says.

When his busy schedule permits, Whatley and his wife have been known to strap their kids on their backs and hike off along a mountain trail. Their daughter, now six, "bagged" three or four ten-thousand-foot summits before she could walk.

Just as humans enjoy Yosemite's great outdoors, some of the park's wildlife find the indoors appealing. As Whatley looked over the dining room one morning, the breakfast tables set with spotless linens and gleaming glassware, he noticed a movement out of the corner of his eye, followed by a loud crash. The Bracebridge ringtail—or one of his offspring—had fallen from a roof truss onto one of the elegantly set tables, a thirty-foot drop, before scampering away. Whatever would Lady Astoria think?

These 1940s-era menus recall the bygone, more slowly-paced days when original menus were printed on site for each meal, every day.

WAWONA HOTEL
Victorian Romance

Long before The Ahwahnee was built to satisfy a celebrated clientele, the Wawona Hotel offered gracious, family-style hospitality to its guests. Four miles inside the south entrance to Yosemite National Park, the Wawona Hotel perches on a hill overlooking a meadow near the south fork of the Merced River. The Wawona's collection of white clapboard buildings is the oldest resort complex in the national park system, a National Historic Landmark, and a member of the National Trust Historic Hotels of America.

The earliest hotel on this site was a log cabin built in 1857 by Galen Clark, the guardian of Yosemite and Mariposa Grove when they were ceded to the state. In 1870 the four Washburn brothers acquired it, and Big Tree Station became a stage stop for freighters and passengers on their way to Yosemite.

The Washburn family ran the hotel for the next sixty years, exploring the area and collecting its legends. They found holes worn into granite rocks along the creek that were made by acorn-grinding Indians. Jean, wife of A. H. "Henry" Washburn, suggested an Indian word, Wah-wo-nah (guardian spirit of the Big Trees), as a more suitable name for the hotel.

Wawona became known for its wooded setting, good meals, and generous hospitality. Often the number of paying guests was equaled by visiting friends and relatives. Famous guests include President Ulysses Grant and his wife, Rutherford B. Hayes, Theodore Roosevelt, and William Jennings Bryan.

After Clark's original buildings burned down, the Washburns added structures with deep porches, verandas, and gables, built in various Victorian styles. The buildings' exterior walls align with the cardinal directions and face the circular driveway and cobblestone fountain, creating an air of formality.

Daily life at Wawona, anything but formal, was a lively blend of stables and smithy, laundry, gardens, lily ponds, wandering peacocks, and children. *Lots* of children. Though Jean and Henry's firstborn died, they raised a nephew's children along with their own daughter. Across the river, Jean's brother had a homestead and seven children. One guest noted this handbill giving away puppies: "A. H. Washburn, five kids and box of dogs!"

This Victorian hotel boasts a full-length front porch where guests have relaxed or played checkers for more than one hundred twenty-five years.

Period decor adds to the romantic setting of Wawona's dining room.

Henry's brother, John, came to California a widower. The local paper noted that he was single and good looking, and wondered why one of the local girls hadn't snared him. A few years later, John met seventeen-year-old Estella Louise Hill, daughter of painter Thomas Hill. At Washburn's generous (and smitten) invitation, Hill built a studio next to the hotel.

John and "Stella" courted, married, and honeymooned in Yosemite, then settled into hotel life. Estella's upright piano stood in the parlor next to the lobby, and nearly every evening she played and sang for hotel guests and friends. She loved flowers and learned the names of local wildflowers, making cards from them to sell in her father's studio.

Hill kept two rowboats, *Honest John* and *Maid of the Mist*, on the nearby pond, which John named Stella's Lake for his bride. Couples still enjoy walking around the pond and gardens on moonlit evenings, and the Wawona is a romantic and popular setting for weddings.

The Wawona's seven buildings, constructed during four decades over the turn of the last century, have a unifying Victorian theme though each building includes elements unique to the time it was built: Stick, Eastlake, Palladian, and Greek Revival. The 1894 Moore Cottage, a favorite of honeymooners, has three tiers with Palladian details and gingerbread ornamentation that makes it look a bit like a wedding cake.

Hill's 1886 studio, vine-draped and decorated with the family's collection of squirrel pelts, dried flowers, rattlesnake skins, and wasps' nests, stood near the fountain. Hill worked here during the summers until his death in 1908. Over the years the studio has been an ice-cream parlor, dance hall, and recreation room, but it has now been restored to its original design.

The hotel's main building, which opened in 1879, has wood doors with transom windows that open onto a two-story veranda. Guestrooms are beautifully furnished with period furniture and block-printed wallpaper, and most of the hotel's hundred-plus guestrooms have veranda doors. All are without telephones or televisions, which means the peaceful setting follows guests inside. Those weary of sightseeing or hiking can sip iced tea on the veranda, meander along the creek or ponds, listen to the piano in the lounge, or golf on a nine-hole course that dates to 1918.

Every Saturday evening throughout the summer, the Wawona hosts an old-fashioned barbecue on the lawn, a nostalgic meal featuring cowboy beans, ribs, burgers, chicken, watermelon, pies, and cakes.

More elegant dining is available in the Wawona's dining room, which is finished in traditional Victorian style with a rustic flair. Two walls have wainscot-to-ceiling windows with large panes separated by narrow mullions. Hand-painted light fixtures embellished with giant sequoia cones hang from the box-beamed ceiling. On warm summer nights, guests can dine on the veranda.

Executive chef Robert Stritzinger's menu emphasizes local, organic, and sustainable items. A local farmer who raises certified organic produce supplies most of Yosemite's hotels. Pantry staples, such as grains and beans, are all organic, as are canned tomatoes from a supplier thirty miles away.

Though he grew up in Michigan, Stritzinger worked in Santa Fe for nine and a half years at La Fonda and the Coyote Café, among other restaurants. Deft with southwestern flavors and ingredients, he often adds a delicious twist to classic dishes, such as Wawona's signature White Turkey Chili (page 67). It's a favorite among guests, many of whom have been making memories here for thirty or forty years, becoming part of the Wawona story.

STEPHEN MATHER
Founding Director of the National Park Service

An avid hiker and mountain climber, Stephen T. Mather went to Washington, D.C., in 1915 as assistant to Secretary of the Interior Franklin Lane. Secretary Lane believed that Mather, a longtime conservationist who had many influential friends, would promote the idea of a national park service as successfully as he had promoted borax years before.

Mather was a former newspaper reporter with no business experience when he convinced borax company executives to advertise their product with the twenty-mule team logo. Promoted to executive himself, he made a fortune before turning to public service.

In one apocryphal tale (a story his assistant, Horace Albright, later declared untrue), Mather came by his position with the Department of the Interior by writing a letter of complaint to Lane highlighting the deplorable conditions in Yosemite. Lane supposedly told Mather that if he didn't like the way the parks were run, he should come to Washington and run them himself.

Whether the tale is true or false, Mather became the founding director of the National Park Service in 1916. He worked tirelessly, visiting each of the parks to identify problem areas, courting the support of wealthy individuals and corporations, at the same time curtailing further exploitation by private interests. He organized a ranger force to replace the army presence, not only to enforce order in the parks but also to greet and educate visitors.

His efforts were remarkably successful, but the stress of that first year took its toll. Overcome by self-doubt, Mather suffered a period of depression so devastating that assistant director Horace Albright took over until Mather could return in 1919. Mather continued his advocacy for the parks until he retired in 1929, a year before his death.

The Sierra Club called him "an ardent and lovable comrade." A brass plaque honoring Mather hangs in the Ranger Club at Yosemite, a handsome rustic chalet (now a National Historic Landmark) that Mather paid for out of his own pocket in 1920.

FISCALINI FARMS CHEDDAR CHEESE SOUP
and Sierra Nevada Pale Ale

AHWAHNEE HOTEL

6 slices of bacon, chopped

1 tablespoon butter

½ cup finely diced onion

1 tablespoon minced garlic

½ cup all-purpose flour

1 ½ quarts Roasted Vegetable Broth

2 cup heavy cream

2 tablespoons Worcestershire sauce

2 tablespoons Dijon mustard

2 teaspoons prepared horseradish

2 bay leaves

Salt and pepper

1 (12-ounce) bottle Sierra Nevada Pale Ale

2 cups shredded Fiscalini Farms Cheddar cheese
(or your favorite Cheddar)

Sourdough croutons

Heat a large stockpot and add the diced bacon. Cook until the bacon is about two-thirds done. Add the butter, onion, and garlic and continue cooking for 3 minutes, or until the onions are translucent.

Stir in the flour to make a roux and cook, stirring, another 3 minutes. Slowly whisk in the vegetable stock and heavy cream until they are incorporated. Bring to a boil and add the Worcestershire sauce, mustard, horseradish, and bay leaves. Reduce heat and simmer for 20 minutes. Add the ale and Cheddar cheese, whisking soup until it is smooth and all the cheese has melted.

Remove the bay leaves and discard. Add salt and pepper to taste. Garnish with Sourdough Croutons before serving.

Makes 8 servings

ROASTED VEGETABLE BROTH

2 cups coarsely chopped onions

2 cups coarsely chopped leeks, washed thoroughly

2 cups coarsely chopped celery

2 cups coarsely chopped carrots

2 cups coarsely chopped parsnips

2 cups coarsely chopped tomatoes

4-5 cloves garlic, crushed

¼ cup vegetable oil

4 ½ quarts cold water

Herb-spice sachet (see note)

Kosher salt

Preheat the oven to 400 degrees F. Toss the onions, leeks, celery, carrots, parsnips, tomatoes, and garlic in oil. Arrange the vegetables in a shallow pan and roast them, turning frequently, until all exposed surfaces are browned.

Place the roasted vegetables in a stockpot, add water and sachet, and simmer for 30 to 40 minutes. Remove the sachet and discard it. Strain the stock through a fine sieve. Adjust seasonings as needed.

Makes 1 gallon

SOURDOUGH CROUTONS

1 sourdough baguette

2 tablespoons clarified butter

2 tablespoons olive oil

4 cloves garlic, crushed

¼ cup chopped parsley

½ cup finely grated Parmigiano-Reggiano cheese

Salt and pepper

Preheat the oven to 350 degrees F. Remove the crust from the bread and cut bread into small cubes.

Heat the clarified butter and olive oil in a large skillet over medium heat. Add the garlic and sauté lightly to perfume the oil-butter blend, then discard the garlic. Add the bread cubes, tossing lightly. Stir in the parsley and cheese, coating all bread cubes evenly. Season to taste with salt and pepper.

Arrange seasoned bread cubes in a single layer on a baking sheet. Bake until golden brown, approximately 12 minutes.

Makes about 4 cups

ROASTED GRANNY APPLE BISQUE
with Apple-Ginger Compote and Curry Crème Fraîche

AHWAHNEE HOTEL

1 pound Granny Smith apples, peeled, cored, and diced

2 tablespoons butter

½ cup diced onions

¼ cup diced celery

¼ cup diced parsnip

¼ cup diced leek, white part only

1 teaspoon minced garlic

1 ½ quarts vegetable stock

½ cup white wine

¼ cup apple cider vinegar

½ cup heavy cream

2 cinnamon sticks

¼ teaspoon ground cardamom

¼ teaspoon ground coriander

1 teaspoon chopped fresh thyme

2 bay leaves

¼ cup long grain white rice

½ teaspoon white pepper

2 teaspoons salt

Apple-Ginger Compote

Curry Crème Fraîche

Preheat oven to 350 degrees F. Melt 1 tablespoon of the butter over medium heat. Place the apples in a mixing bowl, add melted butter, tossing to coat. Spread the apples evenly on a sheet pan and roast for 30 minutes, or until lightly caramelized. Remove and cool slightly.

Melt the remaining 1 tablespoon of butter in a stockpot. Add onions, celery, parsnip, leek, and garlic, cooking until onions are translucent. Add apples, stock, wine, vinegar, cream, cinnamon, cardamom, coriander, thyme, and bay leaves. Bring the mixture to a simmer and add rice, stirring constantly. Cover and simmer for 30 minutes over medium-low heat, stirring occasionally. Remove from heat and allow to cool slightly.

Remove the cinnamon sticks and bay leaves. Purée the soup in batches, filling the blender halfway for each batch. Start on low speed, increasing to high speed, and blending until smooth. (Alternatively, this can be done with an immersion blender.) Strain the soup through a fine strainer into a clean stock pot. Add salt and pepper, adjusting seasonings to taste. Reheat soup over low heat and keep warm until serving.

Garnish each bowl of soup with a generous spoonful of Apple-Ginger Compote (page 59), topped with a dollop of Curry Crème Fraîche.

Makes 8 servings

APPLE-GINGER COMPOTE

AHWAHNEE HOTEL

1 cup Granny Smith apples, peeled, cored, and diced
1 tablespoon minced ginger
¼ cup apple cider vinegar
¼ cup brown sugar
1 whole cinnamon stick
¼ cup water
Pinch of salt

Combine the apples, ginger, vinegar, sugar, cinnamon, water, and salt in a small saucepan and cook for 30 minutes. Add more water as needed to prevent burning. The final consistency should be jam-like, and the apples should be soft. Keep at room temperature and use to garnish Roasted Granny Apple Bisque (page 58).

Makes 1 cup

CURRY CRÈME FRAÎCHE

AHWAHNEE HOTEL

½ cup crème fraîche (or substitute sour cream)
1 teaspoon curry powder
Pinch of salt
Pinch of sugar

Mix crème fraîche, curry, salt, and sugar in a small bowl until thoroughly blended. Use to garnish Roasted Granny Apple Bisque.

Makes ½ cup

WHITE BEAN–ARTICHOKE SPREAD

AHWAHNEE HOTEL

1 head garlic

1 teaspoon olive oil

¾ cup cooked white beans

¼ cup chopped artichoke bottoms

¼ teaspoon chopped fresh tarragon leaves

¼ teaspoon chopped fresh thyme leaves

Preheat oven to 400 degrees F. Cut off the top of the head of garlic. Place the garlic on a 12-inch square piece of aluminum foil, drizzle garlic with olive oil, and fold foil up the sides of the garlic to create a purse. Bake for 45 minutes. Cool. Squeeze each clove to remove the roasted garlic. Set aside 1 teaspoon of garlic to make spread. Use the remainder for toasted sourdough, pasta, salads, mashed potatoes, et cetera.

Place 1 teaspoon of roasted garlic in a food processor with beans, artichoke bottoms, tarragon, and thyme. Purée until smooth. For extra-smooth purée, push bean mixture through a strainer using a rubber spatula or the back of a kitchen spoon. Serve with bread or crackers.

Makes 1 cup

PONZU

AHWAHNEE HOTEL

1 cup mirin or other rice wine

1 kaffir lime leaf

2 slices ginger

¼ cup soy sauce

1 teaspoon red pepper flakes

1 teaspoon nori flakes

2 tablespoons fresh lemon juice

Combine the mirin, kaffir lime leaf, and ginger in a small saucepan. Bring to a boil and reduce to ⅓ cup. Cool. Whisk in the soy sauce, lemon juice, red pepper flakes, and nori flakes. Refrigerate overnight. Strain through a fine mesh sieve before serving.

Makes ¾ cup

CRABMEAT GYOZA
with Ponzu and Sweet Chile Dipping Sauce

AHWAHNEE HOTEL

1 tablespoon sesame oil

½ cup minced onion

1 tablespoon minced ginger

1 tablespoon minced garlic

½ pound crabmeat, picked clean of shells

¼ cup mayonnaise

2 eggs, lightly beaten

2 cups white bread crumbs

2 tablespoons soy sauce

1 teaspoon Thai Sriracha chile sauce*

2 tablespoons finely chopped cilantro

¼ cup finely sliced scallions

2 tablespoons cornstarch

2 tablespoons water

1 package gyoza (60 wrappers)

1 tablespoon vegetable oil

1 cup water

Ponzu

Sweet Chile Dipping Sauce

Heat the sesame oil in a skillet and slowly sauté the onion until it starts to caramelize. Add the ginger and garlic and cook briefly. Cool.

Combine the crabmeat, mayonnaise, eggs, bread crumbs, soy sauce, chile sauce, cilantro, and scallions, mixing thoroughly. Refrigerate up to 24 hours, until ready to assemble the gyoza.

Mix the cornstarch and water. Use it to moisten the edges of the gyoza wrappers, a few at a time. Place 1 tablespoon of filling in the center of each wrapper. Fold in half and seal the edges. Arrange on a sheet pan lightly dusted with cornstarch to prevent sticking. Cover with a slightly damp paper towel until all the gyoza are assembled.

Heat the vegetable oil over medium-low heat in a large, heavy-bottomed pan with a tight fitting lid. Working quickly, arrange the gyoza in the pan until it is full. When the gyoza are golden brown on the bottom, add water. Cover, reduce heat to low, and cook for about 10 minutes, until the water is evaporated and gyoza are done. Serve with Ponzu (page 60) and Sweet Chile Dipping Sauce (page 63).

Makes 8 servings

If Thai Sriracha chile sauce is unavailable, substitute ½ teaspoon Tabasco.

GRILLED KOBE BEEF TRI-TIP
with Upland Cress

1 Kobe beef tri-tip roast, about 2 ¼ to 2 ½ pounds

2 tablespoons kosher salt

1 tablespoon coarsely ground black pepper

¼ pound upland cress or watercress

Lavender-Sweet Corn Custard

Roasted Shallot Demi-Glace

Prepare a gas or charcoal grill. Trim the fat from the beef. Season the roast generously with salt and pepper. Set aside at room temperature for 45 minutes. This prepares the roast to cook more evenly under the intense heat of the grill, and allows the salt to soak into the meat for added flavor.

Grill the roast, turning occasionally (about every 5 minutes) for 20 minutes. Remove from the grill and set aside for 10 minutes prior to slicing. Thinly slice the roast against the grain. Serve with upland cress, Lavender-Sweet Corn Custard, and Roasted Shallot Demi-Glace (page 63).

Makes 6 to 8 servings

LAVENDER-SWEET CORN CUSTARD   AHWAHNEE HOTEL

2 eggs, beaten

1 cup milk

1 tablespoon sugar

1 teaspoon salt

⅛ teaspoon pepper

1 tablespoon dried lavender flowers

2 ears of white sweet corn
(or enough to make 2 cups of kernels)

Preheat the oven to 350 degrees F. Combine the eggs, milk, sugar, salt, and pepper in a large bowl. Add the lavender and corn, mixing well. Pour into a buttered 1½-quart casserole dish or individual ramekins. Place the casserole or ramekins in a cake pan and carefully add water to halfway up the sides of the casserole.

Bake for 40 minutes (25 minutes for ramekins), until custard is set and done in the center.

Makes 6 to 8 servings

ROASTED SHALLOT DEMI-GLACE

1 tablespoon butter

1 tablespoon thinly sliced shallots

2 tablespoons red wine

1 cup veal stock

1 cup brown sauce

Salt and pepper

Melt the butter in a medium saucepan. Add shallots and cook on medium heat, stirring occasionally until caramelized, about 10 minutes.

Deglaze the pan with red wine and cook until the liquid is reduced by half. Add stock and brown sauce and return to a simmer. Continue cooking until reduced by half, skimming any foam from the surface and sides of the pan. This process may take approximately 2 hours. Most of the impurities will be removed, and the sauce should be the consistency of cold heavy cream.

Keep the sauce warm until ready to serve. This sauce can also be refrigerated for up to 5 days, or frozen in ice cube trays for future use.

Makes 1 cup

SWEET CHILE DIPPING SAUCE

¼ cup water

¼ cup sugar

1 teaspoon salt

½ cup rice wine vinegar, unseasoned

1 teaspoon sambal oelek*

Combine the water and sugar in a small pan and bring to a boil. Cook until the sugar is dissolved and mixture is reduced slightly. Remove from heat and add vinegar, salt, and sambal oelek. Refrigerate several hours or overnight.

Makes ¾ cup

Look for sambal oelek, a sweet chile sauce, in Indian or Asian markets.

SCALLOP AND SHIITAKE MUSHROOM WELLINGTON

AHWAHNEE HOTEL

¾ cup sliced shallots

¼ cup (½ stick) butter

2 tablespoons sugar

Salt and pepper

16 scallops, cleaned and sliced in half crosswise

16 shiitake mushroom caps, seasoned and roasted

1 egg

2 tablespoons water

8 egg roll wrappers, cut in half

Oil for deep-frying

8 cups loosely packed spinach leaves

1 cup Truffle Vinaigrette

Plum Tomato Confit

Place the shallots, butter, and sugar in a large skillet and slowly caramelize over medium-low heat, stirring occasionally, until mixture is a dark golden-brown. Cool.

Season the scallops with salt and pepper. Assemble eight Napoleon-style stacks in layers, beginning with a half scallop. Continue building each stack with a mushroom cap, another half scallop, and a spoonful of the caramelized shallots.

Whisk the egg and water to make an egg wash. Wrap each stack with half an egg roll wrapper. Brush the edges of the wrapper with the egg wash and loosely close the sides of the wrapper.

Heat the oil in a fryer or deep skillet to 350 degrees F. Deep-fry the scallop bundles for 3 minutes, or until golden brown. Remove and slice each bundle in half exposing the Napoleon inside.

Toss the spinach leaves with Truffle Vinaigrette (page 65) and place on eight individual plates or a large platter. Arrange the scallops over the spinach and garnish with Plum Tomato Confit.

Makes 8 servings

PLUM TOMATO CONFIT

1 cup extra-virgin olive oil

2 basil leaves

2 cloves garlic, bruised

1 thyme sprig

3 black peppercorns

4 tomatoes, peeled, seeded, and cut into quarters

Heat the oil in a skillet and add basil, garlic, thyme, and peppercorns. Cook over medium heat for 15 minutes to infuse the oil. Pour the hot oil over the tomatoes and let stand for 20 minutes. Cut each tomato quarter in half, making 32 pieces (4 per portion).

Makes 8 servings

TRUFFLE VINAIGRETTE

5 tablespoons vegetable oil

1 tablespoon diced shallots

1 tablespoon red wine

1 tablespoon red wine vinegar

¼ teaspoon dried Dijon mustard

½ ounce fresh or canned truffles, chopped

½ ounce truffle oil

1 teaspoon chopped fresh tarragon

Pinch of salt

Pinch of black pepper

Heat the oil in a small skillet and cook shallots until translucent. Add red wine and reduce by half. Add the red wine vinegar, mustard, and truffles, whisking to incorporate. Slowly whisk in the truffle oil. Season with tarragon, salt, and pepper. Serve immediately or store in the refrigerator for up to 3 days.

Makes ½ cup

CHARRED AND PEPPERED SALMON CLUB

AHWAHNEE HOTEL

1 medium cucumber, peeled, seeded, and thinly sliced (about ½ cup)

1 teaspoon minced fresh dill

½ teaspoon sugar

2 tablespoons rice wine vinegar

1 teaspoon vegetable oil

Salt and pepper

1 large tomato

1 pound fresh salmon cut into 8 fillets

1 tablespoon coarsely ground black pepper

Sea salt

8 very thin slices of serrano ham or prosciutto

8 slices of sourdough bread

Butter

1 cup pea shoots

Toss the cucumbers slices with dill, sugar, vinegar, and vegetable oil. Season to taste with salt and pepper. Refrigerate until ready to use.

Carefully remove the vine end of the tomato with a sharp paring knife. Score the opposite end in an X-shape. Plunge the tomato into boiling water for 30 seconds, or until the skin starts to peel back easily, then submerge the tomato in an ice bath until it is cool enough to handle. Remove the peel and slice the tomato into eight thin slices.

Prepare a grill. Arrange the salmon on a platter, season with salt, and generously coat one side of each fillet with black pepper. Quickly sear the fillets (2 to 3 seconds), pepper side first, then turn over. Repeat the process until all the salmon has been cooked.

Preheat the oven broiler. Arrange the ham on a baking sheet, place under the broiler, and cook until ham is crisp. Brush bread slices with butter and broil until lightly browned.

Place 4 pieces of grilled sourdough bread on a clean work surface. Drain the cucumbers, and distribute them equally among the bread slices. Place seared salmon fillets on top of the cucumbers. Top with pea shoots, tomato slices, and ham. Cover with remaining slices of bread and insert picks to hold sandwiches together. Slice each in half. Serve with pickled vegetables or pasta salad.

Makes 4 servings

WHITE TURKEY CHILI

WAWONA HOTEL

1 tablespoon vegetable oil

2 large onions, diced

2 ½ pounds diced turkey breast

5 cloves garlic, minced

2-3 jalapeños, seeded and minced

1 ½ teaspoons toasted ground cumin

1 teaspoon ground New Mexico chile

½ teaspoon ground coriander

½ teaspoon ground white pepper

Roux made with ¼ pound (1 stick) butter and ⅔ cup flour, cooled

2 quarts turkey broth (or substitute chicken broth)

5 poblano chiles, roasted, peeled, seeded, and diced

4 (14-ounce) cans white hominy

1 tablespoon Tabasco, chipotle style

¾ pound fresh tomatoes, diced

1 pound tomatillos, husked and diced

¾ teaspoon salt, or to taste

Shredded cheese, fresh cilantro, lime wedges, and diced red onion for garnish

Heat the oil in soup pot and sauté onions. Add the turkey and sauté until browned. Add garlic and jalapeños and cook 5 more minutes. Add the cumin, chile, coriander, and white pepper, stirring to mix thoroughly. Add the roux and cook until heated through. Add half of the stock and bring to a boil, stirring constantly. Add the remaining stock, poblano chiles, hominy, Tabasco, tomatoes, and tomatillos. Simmer 20 minutes, or until chili has thickened slightly. Season with salt.

Offer guests a selection of garnishes, such as shredded cheese, fresh cilantro, lime wedges, and diced red onion. Serve with warm flour tortillas.

Makes 8 servings

BOYSENBERRY PIE

AHWAHNEE HOTEL

2 tablespoons butter

1 ¼ cups shortening

1 cup bread flour

2 cups pastry flour

1 ¼ teaspoon sugar

1 ¼ teaspoon salt

¾ cup milk

3 pints boysenberries

1 ¼ cups sugar

3 tablespoons Instant Clear Gel

½ teaspoon salt

Additional sugar for crust

Mix the butter and shortening in a large bowl. Add the flours and mix until just combined. Add sugar, salt, and milk, again mixing until just combined. Do not over-mix. Refrigerate.

Preheat the oven to 425 degrees F. Cook boysenberries in a small saucepan over low heat until the berries start to break down. Remove the berries from the heat and strain the juice into a separate bowl. Add the sugar, Instant Clear Gel, and salt, mixing thoroughly. Add the juice back to the berries, stirring lightly.

Divide the dough in half. On a well-floured surface, roll the first dough half into a circle and place it in a 9-inch pie pan. Fill it with an even mound of berry filling. Lightly brush water around the top edge.

Roll out the remaining half of the dough to make the top crust. Set the top crust over the filling and gently press the crust from the center to the edges until it is flush with the filling.

Trim excess dough with a sharp knife, making a raised edge around the circumference of the pie. Pinch this edge to give it a fluted appearance. Lightly brush the top crust with water and sprinkle with additional sugar. Bake until golden brown.

Makes 1 (9-inch) pie

STRAWBERRY–POPPY SEED SHORTCAKE
with Grand Marnier Whipped Cream

AHWAHNEE HOTEL

POPPY SEED SHORTCAKE

1 cup flour

½ teaspoon salt

1 ½ tablespoons baking powder

2 tablespoons poppy seeds

Zest of ½ orange

½ stick chilled butter, cut into pieces

1 ⅝ cups heavy cream

1 egg

2 tablespoons water

Granulated sugar

STRAWBERRY SAUCE

2 pints strawberries, cleaned

½ cup sugar

GRAND MARNIER WHIPPED CREAM

4 cups chilled heavy cream

¾ cup sugar

2 tablespoons vanilla extract

4 tablespoons Grand Marnier

In a mixer with a paddle attachment, combine the flour, salt, baking powder, poppy seeds, orange zest, and butter. Mix until the dough appears sandy and just begins to clump on the side of the bowl. Add the cream and mix until just combined.

Roll out the dough on a floured surface to 1 inch thick, occasionally lifting it up from underneath to allow the dough to relax. Cut the dough into circles and let them rest on a baking sheet for about an hour.

Preheat oven to 350 degrees F. Beat together the egg and water to make a wash. Brush the dough with egg wash and sprinkle generously with granulated sugar. Bake until golden brown, about 15 minutes.

For strawberry sauce, reserve approximately a quarter of the berries. Purée the remaining berries and sugar in a food processor. Quarter the reserved berries and stir them into the strawberry purée.

To make the whipped cream, chill a mixing bowl in the freezer until it is cold. Pour the cold cream into the chilled mixing bowl and whip it with a mixer until it thickens. Mix in sugar, vanilla, and Grand Marnier. Top each biscuit with strawberry sauce and a dollop of Grand Marnier Whipped Cream.

Makes 12 servings

KEY LIME ICE-BOX CHEESECAKE
with Pistachio Crust

AHWAHNEE HOTEL

2 cups shelled pistachios

¾ cup sugar, divided in half

¼ cup melted butter, more as needed

1 ½ cups heavy cream

1 ¼ cups cream cheese, softened

6 ½ ounces white chocolate, melted

6 tablespoons Key lime juice

1 sheet gelatin, softened in ice water

Finely grind the pistachios and half of the sugar in a food processor. Add the melted butter and process briefly. Test consistency by squeezing some of the mixture in your hand. If it does not hold its shape, add more melted butter until it does. Press firmly into the bottom of a springform pan.

Using a mixer, whip the cream on medium speed until peaks form. Refrigerate. Combine cream cheese and the remaining half of the sugar, mixing on medium speed. Gradually add the white chocolate, mixing on low speed. Scrape the bowl and mix again until smooth.

Use a double boiler over low heat to melt the softened gelatin in the lime juice. Cool slightly and add to the cream cheese mixture, stirring until blended.

Gradually fold the cream cheese mixture into the chilled whipped cream. Pour into the crust and refrigerate at least 2 hours before serving.

Makes 8 servings

WASSAIL PUNCH

AHWAHNEE HOTEL

1 quart apple juice

1 quart cranberry juice

5 tablespoons port

4 whole cloves

1 star anise seed

1 tablespoon dried hibiscus flowers

Rind from half an orange rind, dried

1 cinnamon stick

½ tablespoon grated fresh ginger

Combine the apple juice, cranberry juice, and port in a large pot. Add the cloves, anise, hibiscus, orange rind, and cinnamon. Heat until simmering and continue to simmer for 30 minutes. Serve warm in a coffee mug. Don't forget to sing wassail!

Makes 2 quarts

AVOCADO AIOLI

WAWONA HOTEL

2 avocados, mashed

1 tablespoon lime juice

1 small poblano chile, roasted, peeled, and seeded

2 tablespoons minced cilantro

3 tablespoons mayonnaise

Salt

Place the avocados, lime juice, chile, cilantro, and mayonnaise in a food processor. Purée until smooth. Season to taste with salt.

Makes about 2 cups

BÉCHAMEL SAUCE

WAWONA HOTEL

¼ cup (½ stick) unsalted butter

¼ cup flour

1 quart milk

2 cups grated Parmesan cheese

Small pinch of nutmeg

Melt the butter in a small, heavy-bottomed pot. Stir in the flour to make a roux. Cook for about 3 minutes, until mixture begins to smell nutty. Slowly add the milk, stirring until it reaches a low boil and thickens slightly. Remove from heat and stir in the Parmesan and nutmeg.

Makes about 5 cups

CORN AND POTATO HASH

WAWONA HOTEL

2 russet potatoes, peeled and diced*

Vegetable oil

1 small red bell pepper, diced*

2 poblano chiles, peeled, seeded, and diced*

½ medium onion, diced*

1 cup corn

1 teaspoon fresh minced oregano
(or substitute chives, cilantro, or sage)

2 tablespoons olive oil

Blanch the potatoes in boiling water about 7 minutes, until just cooked through. Drain.

Coat the bottom of a medium skillet with vegetable oil and sauté the onions and bell peppers for 5 minutes. Add corn and sauté 3 minutes more. Remove from heat. Add poblano chiles and potatoes, mixing well. Recipe can be prepared to this point up to 2 days ahead.

Heat olive oil in a medium skillet until it is hot but not smoking. Add vegetable hash and sauté until lightly browned.

Makes 4 servings

This recipe works best when the vegetables are diced about the size of a corn kernel.

SPINACH AND MUSHROOM LASAGNA

WAWONA HOTEL

¾ cup sun-dried tomatoes

1 small onion, diced

1 tablespoon olive oil

¼ pound button mushrooms, sliced

¼ pound portobello mushroom caps, sliced

¼ pound shiitake mushroom caps, sliced

1 teaspoon minced garlic

½ cup marsala

½ minced teaspoon fresh thyme

1 ½ pound spinach, cleaned

½ teaspoon kosher salt

¼ teaspoon pepper

2 (14-ounce) cans artichoke hearts,
drained and coarsely chopped

2 cups ricotta cheese

2 eggs, lightly beaten

1 (8-ounce package) precooked lasagna noodles

1 pound mozzarella cheese, shredded

½ cup grated Parmesan cheese

1 recipe Béchamel Sauce

Roasted Tomato–Bell Pepper Sauce,
pesto, and additional Parmesan for garnish

Cover sun-dried tomatoes with hot water to rehydrate them. about 10 minutes. Drain tomatoes and cut into julienne strips.

Sauté the onion in olive oil until softened. Add mushrooms and sauté until half-cooked. Add the garlic, marsala, and thyme. Cook until mixture is almost dry, then remove from heat.

Wilt the spinach in a dry pan. Cool, squeeze dry, and chop. Combine spinach and mushrooms in a large bowl. Stir in the salt, pepper, artichokes, soaked sun-dried tomatoes, and ricotta cheese. Mix in the eggs, combining well.

Preheat the oven to 350 degrees F. Layer a 9 x 13-inch pan with a fourth of the Béchamel Sauce (page 73), 3 lasagna noodles, half of the mushroom mixture, another fourth of the béchamel, and one-third of the mozzarella.

Continue with 3 more lasagna noodles, the remaining mushroom mixture, another fourth of the béchamel, and another third of the mozzarella. Finish with 3 more noodles, and the rest of the béchamel and mozzarella. Top with parmesan.

Cover with foil and bake 50 minutes. Uncover and bake 10 more minutes. Let rest for 10 minutes before cutting. Cut into 8 pieces. Serve on individual plates topped with Roasted Tomato–Bell Pepper Sauce (page 76), a little pesto, and additional parmesan. Serve with garlic toast.

Makes 8 servings

ROASTED TOMATO–BELL PEPPER SAUCE

12 Roma tomatoes

Salt

Black pepper

Olive oil

2 large red bell peppers

2 tablespoons balsamic vinegar

1 cup olive oil

¾ teaspoon kosher salt, or to taste

½ teaspoon ground white pepper, or to taste

Extra olive oil, salt and black pepper for roasting

Preheat the oven to 400 degrees F. Slice the tomatoes in half lengthwise and place them in a large bowl. Sprinkle lightly with salt and black pepper. Toss with just enough olive oil to coat. Arrange tomatoes on a baking sheet.

Dice bell peppers into 1-inch pieces and place them in a large bowl. Sprinkle lightly with salt and black pepper. Toss with just enough olive oil to coat. Spread onto a baking sheet. Place both pans in the oven and roast until the vegetables are lightly blackened around the edges.

Combine the tomatoes, peppers, and balsamic vinegar in blender. Purée, adding oil slowly to emulsify. Season with salt and white pepper to taste.

Serve sauce over pasta or use in Spinach and Mushroom Lasagna (page 74). It freezes well and can be stored for future use.

Makes about 6 cups

PORT WINE SAUCE   WAWONA HOTEL

2 cups port wine

1 tablespoon sugar

1 teaspoon lemon juice

Boil port wine and sugar in a small pan until reduced to ½ cup. Cool. Stir in lemon juice. Serve with Pine Nut Pie.

Makes ½ cup

SOUTHWESTERN SPICE RUB

WAWONA HOTEL

¾ cup ground New Mexico chile*

¼ cup paprika

1 tablespoon ground white pepper

1 tablespoon Mexican oregano, toasted

1 tablespoon whole coriander, toasted and ground

2 tablespoons cumin seed, toasted and ground

1 tablespoon kosher salt

1 tablespoon sugar

1 teaspoon cayenne

Combine ground chile, paprika, white pepper, oregano, coriander, cumin, salt, sugar, and cayenne, mixing well.

Makes 1½ cups

Ground New Mexico chile is dried and ground chiles with nothing else added. Do not substitute commercial chili powder, as it has other ingredients mixed in.

PINE NUT PIE

WAWONA HOTEL

1 ½ cups sugar

1 cup corn syrup

4 eggs

5 tablespoons melted butter

1 tablespoon vanilla extract

1 cup pine nuts

1 (9-inch) pie shell

Port Wine Sauce, for garnish

Preheat the oven to 300 degrees F. Mix the sugar, corn syrup, eggs, butter, and vanilla. Place the pine nuts in the pie shell. Pour the filling over the nuts and bake 50 to 65 minutes. Cool before serving. Garnish each slice with a drizzle of Port Wine Sauce (page 76).

Makes 8 servings

DEATH VALLEY NATIONAL PARK

For all the toll the desert takes of a man it gives compensations,
deep breaths, deep sleep, and the communion of the stars.
— MARY AUSTIN

INDIANS CALLED THIS PLACE Tomesha—ground afire. At 282 feet below sea level, and receiving fewer than two inches of rain a year with summer temperatures soaring to well over a hundred degrees, Death Valley is the hottest, driest, lowest spot in North America. Yet even here, one can find oases of life.

In spring, splashes of green, gold, and purple flood the washes, hillsides, and roadways when evening primrose, desert gold, phacelia, and other wildflowers burst into bloom. More than a thousand varieties of plants live within the park. Best known for its below-sea-level desert, the park's landscape rises to the summit of Telescope Peak at 11,049 feet. Larger animals, such as the desert bighorn, live in the higher elevations. But even in the low desert, animals roam—or crawl—at night, including more than thirty species of reptiles.

The land itself is colorful, with volcanic and sedimentary hills and long vistas edged by high peaks. Artist's Drive, a nine-mile paved road, winds through rock formations in a palette of desert hues, lavenders, oranges, and golds.

Rumors of a different kind of gold attracted prospectors here in the 1800s. A group of Forty-niners trying to find a shortcut to the Sierra gold fields wandered in this desert for five weeks, leaving behind the name Death Valley. Mining towns gone bust dot the area: Rhyolite, Death Valley Junction, Mosaic Canyon, and Stovepipe Wells Village.

Eventually, the earth did yield riches, but it was borax and not precious metals that created a mining boom. Mines such as Harmony Borax Works supplied borax for porcelain, cosmetics, papermaking, and laundry products. By 1888, Harmony's famed twenty-mule teams had hauled more than twenty million tons of borax to railheads for shipping.

After the mine was sold to Pacific Borax, a young go-getter named Stephen Mather (yes, that Stephen Mather) boosted borax sales with his idea of using the mule team as a logo.

President Herbert Hoover designated the region Death Valley National Monument in 1933. In 1994, when it was re-designated as a national park, Death Valley became the largest national park in the continental United States, encompassing three thousand square miles.

FURNACE CREEK INN
An Oasis in the Desert

In 1927, the Pacific Borax Company built its own oasis, an elegant corporate retreat that was opened to the public as the Furnace Creek Inn the following year. Designed by architect Albert C. Martin, who also designed Los Angeles City Hall, the inn is constructed of adobe bricks handmade by Paiute and Shoshone laborers.

Furnace Creek Inn's mission-style architecture features red tile roofs and balconies with views across the desert salt flats to the Panamint Mountains. The stonework has a Moorish flavor, created from local travertine by a stonemason from Madrid. The lush grounds are alive with plantings of more than a thousand Deglet-Nour date palm trees from Algeria, and water lilies float on stream-fed pools. A seventy-foot swimming pool, built in 1928, is filled by a natural warm spring.

Construction on Furnace Creek Inn lasted nearly a decade, until its completion in 1935. In 1956, the Fred Harvey Company took over the management of the Furnace Creek Inn and nearby Furnace Creek Ranch. Xanterra Parks & Resorts, Inc. currently manages the four-diamond resort, which has been recently renovated to reflect the classic look of the 1930s.

In some respects Furnace Creek Inn is as similar to a national park lodge as a sheik's palace is to a log cabin. Afternoon tea has been a tradition since 1927, and the famed Sunday brunch attracts pilots who fly to the nearby private airstrip for the meal. A newer tradition is the Wine and Beer Lovers weekend occurring annually each fall.

Because of Death Valley's remote location, chef Michelle "Mike" Hansen jokes, "I could feed them anything." Instead, she chooses to offer a blend of continental, southwestern, and Pacific Rim–influenced dishes, from Rattlesnake Empanadas (page 83) to Tuscan Pancetta Soup (page 91).

She enjoys putting together dishes with complex flavor compounds, often training employees to develop their palates by querying them about what they taste and taking the time to explain why she selected particular combinations.

"I'm not a paper chef," she explains.

She also likes making table visits, greeting diners, and talking to them about the food or sharing her enthusiasm for the desert. Hansen loves the open country of Death Valley, where the sunset is a different color every evening, and where she can watch the stars come out from her front porch.

STARRY NIGHTS

The stars have been shining at Furnace Creek Inn since its 1927 debut. It has hosted a long list of Hollywood's brightest, including Claudette Colbert, Bette Davis, John Barrymore, and Jimmy Stewart. More than forty movies and fifteen television shows have been filmed in Death Valley. Ronald Reagan hosted and starred in several episodes of *Death Valley Days*, swhich began as a radio show that had a fourteen-year run before moving to television for another sixteen years.

Movies shot in Death Valley include *The Gun Fighter* (starring Gregory Peck), *King Solomon's Mines* (Deborah Kerr and Stewart Granger), *Escape from Fort Bravo* (William Holden), *Spartacus* (Kirk Douglas), and *One-Eyed Jacks* (Marlon Brando and Karl Malden). Death Valley has represented deserts all the way from the southwestern U.S. and the Middle East to the planet Tatooine in George Lucas's *Star Wars*.

RATTLESNAKE EMPANADAS

1 pound boneless rattlesnake meat*

3 ounces chicken fat or chicken meat to bind mixture

½ cup finely chopped red bell pepper

½ cup finely chopped yellow bell pepper

½ cup finely chopped green bell pepper

½ cup diced nopalitos*

1 tablespoon ground cumin

1 teaspoon salt

1 teaspoon pepper

1 teaspoon granulated garlic

1 teaspoon ground chile

¼ cup lime juice

2 boxes puff pastry sheets, defrosted

⅔ cup shredded Colby cheese

1 egg

2 tablespoons water

Using a meat grinder or food processor, grind the rattlesnake meat and chicken fat together until the mixture looks like ground pork. Heat a large skillet and add meat, peppers, and nopalitos. Sauté for 15 minutes. Add cumin, salt, pepper, garlic, chile, and lime juice. Cook for 15 to 20 minutes longer. Drain and let cool. Stir in shredded cheese.

Preheat oven to 350 degrees F. Spread out the pastry and it cut into 4-inch circles with a biscuit cutter or can. Beat together the egg and water to make an egg wash. Brush the pastry circles with egg wash and place a spoonful of meat mixture in the middle of each. Fold over the pastry and crimp the edges closed with your fingers or a fork. Bake 12 minutes, or until lightly browned.

Serve with salsa, guacamole, or ranch-style dressing. A good wine pairing is Kendall Jackson Sauvignon Blanc.

Makes 12 to 16 empanadas

Look for nopalitos (sliced cactus) in the ethnic food section of your grocery store and rattlesnake meat at a gourmet store or online.

Opposite: Picture windows afford diners a view of the desert landscape.

BREAD PUDDING

10 cups day-old Danish, torn into large pieces

6 eggs

½ cup sugar

1 tablespoon vanilla

Pinch of salt

½ cup chopped dried cranberries or other dried fruit

⅔ cup chopped dates

1 cup milk

FRENCH TOAST BATTER

6 eggs

1 ½ cups milk

½ cup sugar

2 tablespoons vanilla

2 tablespoons orange liqueur (optional)

1 teaspoon cinnamon

¼ teaspoon nutmeg

Pinch of salt

Preheat the oven to 350 degrees F. Mix the bread, eggs, sugar, vanilla, salt, cranberries, dates, and milk in a large bowl. Spoon the mixture into two loaf pans coated with nonstick spray. Bake for 1 hour. Refrigerate or freeze the bread pudding until you are ready to make the French toast. (This can also be served hot as a bread pudding.)

Slice the bread pudding. Mix eggs, milk, sugar, vanilla, liqueur, cinnamon, nutmeg, and salt with a hand mixer. Soak the slices of bread pudding in batter. Heat a nonstick skillet and cook the French toast until done. Serve immediately with butter and fruit or maple syrup.

Makes 10 servings

WESTERN TENDERLOIN HASH

CHILE PASTE

4 pasilla or New Mexico dried chiles

1 tablespoon dried ground chile

1 tablespoon onion powder

1 teaspoon dried cumin

1 tablespoon minced garlic

1 teaspoon lime zest

2 teaspoons lime juice

1 tablespoon oil

HASH

1 tenderloin fillet (about 10 ounces)

4 tablespoons oil

⅔ cup diced red onion

2 ½ cups diced cooked potatoes

1 cup diced bell peppers

⅔ cup diced tomatoes

4 to 6 eggs

4 to 6 tortillas, optional

Make chile paste: Shake seeds from the chiles. Place the chiles in a food processor and grind them to a powder. Add the ground chile, onion powder, and cumin and mix for about 1 minute. Add the minced garlic, lime zest, lime juice, and oil and process until blended. Scrape the sides and mix again until smooth, about 1 minute more.

To make hash, thinly slice or dice the tenderloin. Heat the oil and sauté the tenderloin and onion for 2 minutes. Stir in potatoes, bell pepper, and chile paste. Cook for 3 minutes more. Just before serving, stir in the tomatoes.

Fry the eggs in a nonstick pan to desired doneness. Arrange the eggs on top of hash before serving. Serve with warm tortillas (optional).

Makes 4 to 6 servings

PRICKLY PEAR STICKY BUNS

½ cup dates

1 tablespoon water

1 (12-ounce) jar prickly pear jelly

½ cup chopped pecans

2 sheets Danish Dough (or use commercially prepared frozen dough)

3 tablespoons butter, cut in pieces and softened

2 tablespoons cinnamon sugar

Place the dates and water in blender or food processor and purée. Transfer the date purée to a small bowl and mix with jelly and pecans.

Roll out the Danish Dough (page 88) into two sheets, each sheet 1 inch thick and 8 to 10 inches wide. Spread each with one-third of the date mixture. In a small bowl, toss butter pieces with cinnamon sugar, then scatter them over the dough. Roll up the dough, forming two logs. Chill them in freezer for about 30 minutes.

Remove the chilled dough and slice it into rounds. The dough can be frozen for later use. Coat a baking sheet with nonstick spray. Place the dough circles about 5 to 8 inches apart. Set the dough in a warm spot until it has tripled in size, about 90 minutes.

Preheat the oven to 350 degrees F. Bake 20 to 25 minutes, until golden brown. Serve warm with the remaining date mixture spooned over the top.

Makes 2 dozen

CRISPY CACTUS APPETIZER

Oil for deep-frying

1 (32-ounce) jar nopalitos*

1 cup flour

1 tablespoon Cajun seasoning (or use ground chile, garlic, white pepper, cumin, and paprika)

Salt and pepper

Heat oil in a deep skillet or fryer until very hot. Drain the cactus thoroughly. Combine the flour and seasoning in large bowl. Season with salt and pepper. Toss the cactus in the flour mixture until pieces are thoroughly coated. Shake off excess flour. Fry the pieces in hot oil until they are crispy, about 2 minutes.

Serve immediately with your favorite dipping sauce, such as salsa, guacamole, or prickly pear-jalapeño jelly.

Makes 4 appetizer portions

Look for nopalitos (sliced cactus) in the ethnic food section of your grocery store.

DANISH DOUGH

1 package dry yeast

4 cups sifted flour

1 teaspoon salt

2 tablespoons sugar

½ cup (1 stick) chilled butter

2 eggs, beaten well

¾ cup hot water (105 to 110 degrees F)

1 ½ cups (3 sticks) butter, softened

Follow package directions to activate the yeast. In the meantime, combine flour, salt, and sugar in a large bowl. Cut ½ cup (1 stick) of the butter into the flour mixture until the mixture is crumbly. Stir in the eggs and yeast. Mix thoroughly with hands.

Transfer the dough to a floured surface and knead it until smooth, about 2 minutes. Roll the dough into a ball, cover, and let it rest in the refrigerator for about 30 minutes.

Roll the dough into a rectangle about 1 to 1½ inches thick and 8 to 10 inches wide. Spread with half of the softened butter and fold the dough over two or three times. Repeat. Refrigerate dough for 2 to 24 hours before using.

Makes enough for 2 dozen rolls

SPINACH DIP

1 small yellow onion, minced

2 teaspoons vegetable oil

1 teaspoon minced garlic

1 (8-ounce) package cream cheese, softened

2 cups mayonnaise

½ cup Dijon mustard

¼ cup milk

1 package ranch dressing mix

1 (16-ounce) package frozen chopped spinach, defrosted and drained

1 (5-ounce) can water chestnuts, drained and chopped

1 cup shredded mozzarella

4 dashes of Tabasco

4 dashes of Worcestershire sauce

Salt and pepper

1 large bread round

1 small loaf of French bread, cubed

Heat the oil and sauté the onion about 4 minutes. Add the garlic and cook for 1 minute more. Set aside.

Combine the cream cheese, mayonnaise, mustard, and milk with ranch dressing mix in a food processor or mixing bowl. Blend well. Fold in onion-garlic mixture, spinach, and water chestnuts. Add cheese, Tabasco, and Worcestershire sauce. Season to taste with salt and pepper, if needed. Refrigerate mixture overnight to blend the flavors.

Before serving, hollow out the bread round to a make a bowl. Fill the bread bowl with dip and arrange bread cubes around it.

Makes 5 to 6 cups

SOUTHWEST CHICKEN SALAD

½ pound diced cooked chicken

2 heads romaine lettuce, chopped

⅔ cup shredded cheese of your choice

1 cup diced tomatoes

½ cup red onion, cut into julienne pieces

1 to 2 avocados, diced

1 package ranch-style dressing mix,
prepared according to package directions

¼ cup chipotle-style Tabasco,
or 1 teaspoon chipotle adobe paste

1 cup Corn and Bean Salsa

4 cups crumbled tortilla chips

Toss the chicken, lettuce, cheese, tomatoes, onion, and avocado in a large bowl. Mix the ranch-style dressing with Tabasco. Toss the salad with Corn and Bean Salsa and enough dressing until coated to your taste. Just before serving, add crumbled chips and toss salad again.

Makes 4 servings

CORN AND BEAN SALSA

You will need ¼ cup cherry, apple, or mesquite-flavored wood chips, found in a hardware store or supermarket, to smoke the corn for this salsa.

1 16-ounce package frozen corn

1 16-ounce can black beans (drained and rinsed)

½ cup diced red and green bell peppers

1 tablespoon minced cilantro

Salt and pepper

To smoke the corn, you will need two pans that fit inside one another. The smaller pan needs to be perforated. Place the corn in the perforated pan. Place the wood chips in the bottom of the larger pan. Place the large pan on the stove with the perforated pan on top. Heat on high for about 10 minutes. The wood should be smoking but not flaming. You can do this on a grill outside.

Mix smoked corn with beans, pepper, and cilantro. Refrigerate until ready to use. Corn and Bean Salsa can be frozen for up to two months. Serve with quesadillas, sautéed chicken breasts, or fish.

Makes 5 cups

TUSCAN PANCETTA SOUP

4 ounces pancetta

2 tablespoons olive oil

1 tablespoon butter

5 ½ cups white or yellow onion, cut into julienne pieces

1 tablespoon sugar

2 quarts vegetable, chicken, or beef stock

5 Roma tomatoes, roughly chopped

2 tablespoons brandy or bourbon (optional)

5 large fresh basil leaves, shredded

Salt and pepper

2 cups croutons

²/₃ cup shredded Parmesan cheese

Remove rind from the pancetta and chop the ham into small pieces. Cook in a very hot skillet and until almost crispy. Add oil, butter, and onions and cook, stirring occasionally, until the onion is lightly caramelized. Add sugar and stir for about 3 minutes more.

Add half the stock and bring to a boil. Cook until the liquid is almost gone. Stir in the remaining stock, tomatoes, and basil. Return the mixture to a boil, decrease heat, and simmer for about 20 minutes. Season to taste with salt and pepper.

Just before serving, divide the croutons among individual bowls, add soup, and sprinkle with cheese.

Makes 4 to 6 servings

CARROT-GINGER SOUP

6 cups carrots, roughly chopped

3 cups vegetable stock

1 ¼ teaspoons ground ginger

3 tablespoons honey

¼ teaspoon granulated garlic

Salt and pepper

Sour cream, for garnish

Cook the carrots in vegetable stock until they are very soft. Cool. Purée the carrots in a blender. Add ginger, honey, and garlic. Season to taste with salt and pepper. Blend well.

Chill for 2 hours or up to 5 days. Stir well and garnish with sour cream before serving.

Makes 4 to 6 servings

BRAISED GARLIC CHICKEN

⅓ cup oil

1 whole frying chicken, cut into pieces

Salt and pepper

1 medium yellow onion, diced

1 (16-ounce) jar garlic cloves, or 6 heads of garlic, peeled

2 tablespoons Tabasco

¼ cup Worcestershire sauce

2 cups Captain Morgan rum (important!)

⅔ cup whiskey

2 cups diet or regular cola or a mixture of both

3 cups veal stock or rich brown gravy mix

1 sprig fresh thyme, or ½ teaspoon dried thyme

Heat the oil in a 6-quart saucepan. Season the chicken pieces with salt and pepper. Lightly brown the chicken in oil, about three minutes on each side. Remove the chicken and set aside.

Sauté the onion and garlic cloves in the chicken drippings until onions are translucent. Return the chicken to pot. Add Tabasco, Worcestershire sauce, and rum. Cook for 5 minutes. Add whiskey and soda. (This will foam up.) Cook for 10 minutes. Add stock and thyme.

Cook for 1 to 1½ hours at medium heat, or until chicken starts to fall off the bone. Serve with cheese risotto or horseradish mashed potatoes.

Makes 2 to 4 servings

STUFFED MOJAVE CHICKEN

CHEESE STUFFING

2 tablespoons Boursin

1 cup grated queso blanco (a white Mexican cheese)

2 mild green chiles, chopped (roasted or canned)

1 cup shredded potato

4 shakes of Tabasco

1 ½ tablespoons cumin

½ tablespoon granulated garlic

Salt and pepper

2 chicken breasts with wing bone, about 6 to 8 ounces total

LIME PASTE

1 tablespoon lime juice

1 tablespoon chili powder

1 tablespoon granulated garlic

1 tablespoon onion powder

¾ teaspoon sugar

Pinch of salt

3 tablespoons vegetable oil

Goat cheese cream, for garnish

Salsa, for garnish

Combine the cheeses, chiles, potato, Tabasco, cumin, and the ½ tablespoon of granulated garlic. Season to taste with salt and pepper. Refrigerate for 30 minutes.

Slit the chicken breasts under the wing bones and stuff each one with some of the cheese mixture. Make a paste of the lime juice, chili powder, 1 tablespoon granulated garlic, onion powder, sugar, and salt. Coat the chicken breasts with the paste.

Preheat oven to 400 degrees F. Heat the oil in a large ovenproof skillet and brown the chicken pieces, breast side down, for 2 minutes. Turn the chicken breast side up and bake for 15 minutes.

Garnish with goat cheese cream and salsa. Serve with wild rice. A good wine pairing is Chateau St. Jean Fumé Blanc.

Makes 2 servings

WILD ALASKA SALMON CAKES

1 (8-ounce) salmon fillet

½ cup lemon juice

2 tablespoons sugar

1 tablespoon salt

1 ½ cups water

4 ounces smoked salmon

4 ounces lox (cured salmon)

¼ cup capers

¼ cup minced red onion

¼ cup bread crumbs

1 tablespoon Dijon mustard

1 egg

½ cup mayonnaise

1 teaspoon Tabasco

2 teaspoons Worcestershire sauce

1 tablespoon lemon juice

Salt and pepper

Zesty Mayo

To poach the salmon, preheat the oven to 350 degrees F. Place the salmon fillet in a glass pan and sprinkle it with the lemon juice. Cover with paper towels, then layer sugar and salt over the towels. Slowly drizzle with water without washing away sugar-salt mixture. Bake for 10 to 15 minutes.

Pour off moisture and peel off paper towels. Refrigerate poached salmon up to 3 days. Crumble the salmon before using.

Dice or mince the smoked salmon and lox. Chop the capers lightly. Mix the poached salmon, smoked salmon, lox, capers, onion, bread crumbs, mustard, egg, mayonnaise, Tabasco, Worcestershire sauce, and lemon juice in a medium bowl. Season with salt and pepper. Form the mixture into 2- to 3-inch cakes.

Heat a grill or a sauté pan coated with nontsick spray or vege-table oil. Cook the salmon cakes 2 to 3 minutes on each side. Serve as cakes or on a sandwich roll with avocado and bacon. Serve with Zesty Mayo (page 95).

Makes 4 to 6 servings

CHOCOLATE TRUFFLES

1 ¼ pounds semisweet chocolate

1 cup heavy cream

2 tablespoons Crème de Menthe

3 tablespoons unsalted butter, melted

1 (8-ounce can) cocoa powder

1 pound unsweetened chocolate

Chopped almonds or chocolate cookie crumbs, for garnish

White chocolate, raspberry, or dark chocolate sauce, for garnish

Melt semisweet chocolate in large double boiler. In a separate pot, bring cream to a soft boil. Add Crème de Menthe to hot cream. Combine melted butter, melted chocolate, and hot cream mixture in a large bowl and fold or whisk until evenly mixed. Chill mixture for 24 hours, or until it sets.

Remove the chocolate mixture from refrigerator and scoop it into balls. Roll them in cocoa powder by hand. Place truffles in freezer for 30 minutes, or until they have hardened.

Melt unsweetened chocolate in double boiler. Line a baking sheet with parchment or wax paper. Using a fork, dip truffles in melted chocolate and set on the parchment. Sprinkle them with garnishes and chill them for at least 15 minutes.

To serve, decorate plates with different sauces and arrange the truffles on top. A good wine pairing is Quady's Starboard Port.

Makes 2½ pounds

ZESTY MAYO

1 cup mayonnaise

½ teaspoon horseradish

3 drops Tabasco

2 drops Worcestershire sauce

2 tablespoons relish

1 tablespoon minced onion

1 teaspoon minced garlic

Mix the mayonnaise, horseradish, Tabasco, Worcestershire sauce, relish, onion, and garlic. Zesty Mayo is best when gently warmed in a microwave before using.

Makes 1 cup

CRATER LAKE NATIONAL PARK

*I now look back on this my 76th birthday, and my heart bounds with joy
and gladness, for I realize that I have been the cause of opening up this
wonderful lake for the pleasure of mankind, millions of whom will come and
enjoy and unborn generations will profit by its glories. Money knows no
charm like this and I am the favored one. Why should I not be happy?*

— WILLIAM GLADSTONE STEEL, *1930*

FIRST THE FACTS: Crater Lake is the deepest lake in the U.S., the second deepest in the Western
Hemisphere, and the seventh deepest in the world. Crater Lake's waters plunge nearly two thousand feet, with a surface greater than twenty
square miles and an estimated volume of five trillion gallons.

But what captivates those who see Crater Lake is the beauty of its startling blue waters and forested setting and the geologic drama
that created it. Crater Lake National Park's 182,700 acres, ninety percent of which are designated wilderness, lie within the volcanically
active Cascade Mountains of southern Oregon. The lake's crater is a caldera, a collapsed volcano, formed sometime after Mount Mazama's
eruption about six thousand years ago. Over centuries the caldera filled with water from rain and snow. Because of its purity, the lake is an
intense, clear blue with visibility more than a hundred feet below the surface.

The collapse of the volcano known as Mount Mazama is referred to in local stories. In a version told by the Klamath people, two
chiefs, Llao of the Below World and Skell of the Above World, fought in a battle that destroyed Llao's home, Mount Mazama. Local tribes
considered the lake off limits and didn't speak of it. White prospectors remained unaware of the lake until 1853.

In 1870, a young Kansas man named William Gladstone Steel sat down to eat his lunch, smoothed out the section of newspaper that

The steep banks of the lake are buried in deep snow each winter.

had been wrapped around it, and began reading an article about Crater Lake. Steel decided he would see this unusual lake for himself someday.

Though his family moved to Portland, Oregon, two years later, it was another thirteen years before Steel at last saw the lake that had captured his imagination. It was love at first sight. For the rest of his life, Steel devoted his time, energy, and money toward the creation and management of Crater Lake National Park.

Steel named many area features and participated in scientific surveys, including Clarence Dutton's U.S. Geological Survey in 1886. The crew hauled a half-ton boat up the mountainside and lowered it to the lake. Using a piece of pipe tied to a spool of piano wire, they sounded the lake's depth. (The method was remarkably accurate: Dutton determined a depth of 1,996 feet, only fifty-three feet more than sonar readings taken seventy-two years later.)

Steel also welcomed the conservation movement of the late 1800s. In 1896, Steel guided conservationist John Muir to Crater Lake. Muir called it "the one grand wonder of the region." The men later discussed strategies for protecting the area. Steel's efforts met with success on May 22, 1902, when President Theodore Roosevelt signed the bill designating Crater Lake National Park.

CRATER LAKE LODGE
Rebuilding a Dream

In 1907, Steel formed the Crater Lake Company and offered a tent camp near the lake so that visitors could have shelter and hot meals, but he saw this as a stopgap measure. Steel's ultimate goal was a lodge grand enough for the magnificent setting.

After a long search for a financial backer, Steel partnered with Portland developer Alfred L. Parkhurst. Estimated project costs were five thousand dollars, but Parkhurst hadn't considered the difficulties of getting workers and supplies to the remote building site or the limited construction season at an elevation of seven thousand feet. Costs climbed to thirty thousand dollars, and Parkhurst trimmed corners wherever he could.

Portland architect Raymond Hockenberry designed the lodge using native stone and wood. Stone masonry was used on the ground floor exterior. The shingled jerkinhead roof featured shed dormers and overhanging eaves. Multi-paned windows with arched stone lintels added a romantic air.

But underneath the lovely exterior was a wooden frame. Hockenberry and Parkhurst underestimated the structural support needed to withstand a Cascade winter. During the winter of 1913-14, the roof collapsed under heavy snows.

The roof was repaired, and the four-story lodge opened in the summer of 1915, before completion. Furnishings were spartan. Exterior walls were clad in tarpaper. Guestroom walls were finished with fiberboard. There were no private bathrooms, and a generator provided electricity. Despite less than luxurious accommodations, increasing numbers of visitors arrived.

Lodge operators added rooms and plumbing, with little improvement in the quality of construction. Many rooms remained unfinished. Heavy auto traffic turned the grounds to mud or dust. The Great Depression meant even less investment for the lodge because it was funded privately. However, the grounds saw great improvement when the National Park Service and the Civilian Conservation Corps began an ambitious landscape project for the Rim Village.

The lodge was closed during much of World War II. In 1943, the park service described the lodge as a "fire trap of the worst sort." When the park service acquired Crater Lake Lodge in 1967, the structure was in a state of advanced deterioration, and the agency became caught between considerations to demolish the lodge and public sentiment.

In the spring of 1989, National Park Service engineers pronounced the lodge's Great Hall unsafe, warning that this section could collapse and bring down the rest of the structure with it. The park service had no choice but to close the lodge and make plans for rehabilitating it.

The lodge, built of native stone and wood, still stands after a history filled with adversity.

The rustic 1920s-era ambience includes hardwood floors, reproduction mission furniture, a fireplace (reconstructed from original stones) in the Great Hall, and a dining room overlooking the lake. It's said that the first meal served in the original lodge was Crater Lake trout, descendants of trout that Steel had stocked the lake with years before. Today's diners can expect classic cuisine with a regional touch. Chef Michelle "Mike" Hansen's version of Crème Brûlé (page 107) incorporates one of Oregon's favorite crops, marionberries.

Hansen, who has known since age nine that she wanted to be a chef, started serving up meals for friends and family by age twelve. She grew up working in the family grocery and watching Graham Kerr and Julia Child on television before attending a culinary vocational school.

Hanson spends the snowy Cascade winters at Death Valley's Furnace Creek Inn, where she is also the chef. The contrast doesn't escape her: on one August day, when Death Valley recorded temperatures well over a hundred degrees, Crater Lake Lodge received eight inches of snow.

After nearly two years of planning and design, rehabilitation began in 1991. Other than masonry stones, very little of the original building materials could be reused. By the time the lodge's rehabilitation was completed, in the fall of 1994, the tab topped fifteen million dollars.

Portland architects Fletcher Farr Ayotte incorporated steel supports and up-to-date safety systems as they recreated the ambience—if not the exact materials or design—of the original lodge. The reborn Crater Lake Lodge opened to the public in May of 1995, its mostly new construction and new furnishings creating an atmosphere that felt more authentic and "older" than the original lodge. The extreme dedication to the lodge's restoration is a testament to Steel's original dream.

FIRE AND ICE

The starring attraction of Crater Lake National Park is the lake, set like a jewel in the center of dozens of remnants pointing to the area's fiery past: extinct volcanic cones, fossil fumaroles, lava flows and dikes, islands, and pumice desert.

Mount Mazama erupted about seven thousand years ago, spewing ash all the way to present-day Wyoming. And the volcano is only sleeping. In the last sixty years, a dozen major quakes have hit the region, including a 6.0 quake in 1993. Some vulcanologists estimate that a nearby fault zone could produce a quake of 7.25 on the Richter scale.

Before fire there was ice. Glaciers carved valleys throughout the Cascades during the last ice age, which ended ten thousand years ago. Today, the Crater Lake area is known for heavy snow, forcing the lodge to close during winter months. Average winter snow accumulation is 544 inches. Snow depths of fifteen feet are common, with a record of twenty-one feet in April 1983.

CLAM CHOWDER

4 slices bacon, diced

½ cup diced carrots

1 cup diced onion

⅔ cup diced celery

¼ teaspoon dried oregano

¼ teaspoon dried basil

¼ teaspoon dried thyme

1 teaspoon minced garlic

2 cups clams and clam juice,
combined (fresh, frozen, or canned)

2 ½ quarts heavy cream
(or milk, half-and-half, or a combination)

4 cups diced potatoes

½ cup olive oil

¼ cup Worcestershire sauce

4 dashes of Tabasco

Clam or shrimp stock, as needed

Salt and pepper

½ cup roux*

½ cup brandy (optional)

Bacon, cooked and crumbled, for garnish

Chopped fresh thyme, for garnish

Heat the oil in a large stockpot. Cook the bacon and add carrots, onion, celery, oregano, basil, and thyme. Sauté about 10 minutes, or until onions are clear. Add the garlic and clams and cook about 10 minutes more. Add the cream and bring to a boil.
Add the potatoes and cook on medium heat, stirring occasionally to prevent scorching, about 30 minutes, or until potatoes are tender. Stir in the Worcestershire sauce and Tabasco. Stir in the roux, a little at a time, until soup is thickened. Add the stock as needed for flavor. Season to taste with salt and pepper. Remove soup from heat and stir in brandy. Before serving, garnish with bacon and fresh thyme.

Makes 10 servings

To make roux, melt 1 cup (2 sticks) butter and stir in 1 cup flour to make a paste. This can be refrigerated for up to a month and used to thicken soups and sauces.

FRENCH ONION SOUP

½ cup vegetable oil

4 large yellow onions, cut into julienne pieces

2 leeks, thinly sliced

½ cup brandy or whiskey

1 gallon beef stock

1 chicken bouillon cube

1 bay leaf

1 clove garlic, minced

1 tablespoon fennel seed

2 tablespoons Worcestershire sauce

1 teaspoon black pepper

Salt

Croutons or crisp-toasted bread

Cheese of your choice

Heat the oil in a large ovenproof pan over high heat. Add the onions and leeks. Cook, stirring, until caramelized. Deglaze the pan with brandy or whiskey, cooking off the liquid. Add one-third of the stock, bouillon cube, bay leaf, garlic, and fennel seed. Cook until reduced by half. Add another third of the stock, Worcestershire sauce, and black pepper. Reduce by half again. Add the remaining stock and bring to a boil. Add salt, if needed. Serve topped with croutons and cheese.

Makes 4 servings

GOUDA CREAM SAUCE

2 quarts heavy cream

3 cups shredded smoked Gouda

½ cup grated Parmesan

1 teaspoon paprika

1 teaspoon minced garlic

1 teaspoon onion powder

2 dashes of Tabasco

2 dashes of Worcestershire sauce

Salt and pepper

Heat the cream in a large saucepan until just before it reaches boiling. Add cheeses, paprika, garlic, onion powder, Tabasco, and Worcestershire sauce. Stir constantly until cheese is fully melted. Do not boil. Season to taste with salt and pepper.

Use immediately over pasta or chicken, or refrigerate for up to 7 days. Sauce can be stored in the freezer for 2 months.

Makes 2 quarts

GRILLED ARTICHOKES

4 artichokes

2 cups olive oil

5 cloves garlic, chopped

Trim a quarter-inch off the top of each artichoke. Cut artichokes in half and steam them for 20 minutes. Meanwhile, heat the olive oil to 100 degrees. Remove from heat and add garlic.

When the artichokes are done, plunge them in ice water for 5 minutes. Drain. Remove them from water and place in a deep pan. Pour the garlic-oil mixture over the artichokes and let them marinate for 2 to 12 hours.

Prepare a grill. Grill artichokes for 1 to 2 minutes on each side. Serve with a dipping sauce, such as Crater Lake's Blue Cheese Mayo (equal amounts of blue cheese dressing and mayonnaise) or Garlic Mayo (sautéed garlic mixed with mayonnaise and lemon juice).

Makes 8 servings

MARIONBERRY CRÈME BRÛLÉE

SAUCE

2 pints marionberries (or berry of your choice)

½ cup sugar

1 tablespoon butter

3 cups water

Pinch of salt

CUSTARD

2 ½ cups heavy cream

1 tablespoon vanilla or a scraped vanilla bean

15 egg yolks

½ cup sugar

Pinch of salt

1 cup of Marionberry Syrup

Sugar for topping

Combine 1½ pints of the berries with sugar, butter, water, and salt in a saucepan. Bring to a boil and cook until mixture is reduced by just over half. Set aside to cool. (This step can be completed up to 5 days ahead.)

Bring the cream and vanilla to a simmer. Set aside to steep, about 10 minutes.

Mix the egg yolks with the ½ cup sugar, salt, and Marion Berry Syrup (page 108), stirring until sugar is dissolved.

Add warm (not hot) cream mixture to egg mixture a little bit at a time, folding in thoroughly and quickly to avoid making berry-scrambled eggs.

Preheat the oven to 325 degrees F. Place reserved berries in the bottoms of 6 to 8 individual ramekins or a large casserole, preferably glass. Gently pour the custard over the berries to about ¼ inch from the top edge of the ramekins or casserole. Place ramekins or casserole in a baking pan and add water to about ½ inch deep. Carefully place pan in oven. Check after 45 minutes. If brûlée jiggles, cook for about 15 minutes longer. Custard is done when it is starting to brown.

Remove the custard from the oven to cool, then refrigerate. Just before serving, preheat the broiler. Sprinkle the custard heavily with sugar. Set the custard very close to the broiler or use a mini blow torch to make a firm sugar crust, watching closely so that the crust does not burn.

Makes 6 to 8 servings

MARIONBERRY DRESSING

3 cups Marionberry Syrup

1 cup balsamic vinegar

1 teaspoon minced garlic

2 tablespoons Dijon mustard

¼ teaspoon dried basil

¼ teaspoon dried oregano

3 to 4 cups olive or salad oil

Salt and pepper

Strain the syrup. Blend with vinegar, garlic, mustard, basil, and oregano. Slowly add oil, whisking in a little at a time, until thickened. (You might not need all the oil.) Season to taste with salt and pepper. Dressing can be refrigerated for up to 2 months.

Makes 8 cups

MARIONBERRY SYRUP

1 pint raspberries, cleaned

1 pint blueberries, cleaned

4 pint marionberries, cleaned

1 pint strawberries, cleaned, stems removed

2 cups sugar

1 tablespoon butter

1 teaspoon salt

2 quarts water

Combine the berries, sugar, butter, salt, and water in a large pot. Bring to a boil and cook for about 2 hours, until reduced by half. Cool and purée with an immersion mixer or blender. Sauce can be frozen for up to 3 months before using. Use over ice cream, desserts, pancakes, et cetera, or make into Marionberry Dressing.

Makes 1 gallon

GARDEN PHYLLO LASAGNA

4 large portobello mushrooms

1 zucchini

1 yellow squash

1 eggplant

1 cup melted butter or olive oil

Salt and pepper

1 (16-ounce) package phyllo dough

5 cups mixed shredded cheeses
(e.g., Parmesan, mozzarella, Cheddar, Jack)

1 (12-ounce) jar roasted red peppers

6 slices provolone or smoked Gouda

6 cups fresh spinach

1 onion, diced

Preheat the oven to 350 degrees F. Remove mushroom stems and scrape out the black ribs on the underside of the caps. Thinly slice zucchini, yellow squash, and eggplant, cutting on the bias. Toss vegetables with a tiny bit of the melted butter and season with salt and pepper. Place them in an ovenproof pan and roast for 10 minutes. Set vegetables aside to cool.

Unfold the phyllo dough and cut it into six even squares. Spread a little of the melted butter on a baking sheet. On the baking sheet, make 6 stacks of 5 sheets of dough each. Spread each stack with more of the butter. Fit the first stack into a casserole dish. On top of this stack layer the mushrooms caps and 5 more sheets of dough. Spread with a little more butter. Layer with ½ of cup spinach, a little more than ½ cup of shredded cheese, and 5 more sheets of dough. Spread with a little more butter. Layer with a piece of red pepper, a slice of Gouda cheese, and more dough. Butter the dough and layer with zucchini, shredded cheese, and more dough. Layer with yellow squash and eggplant.

Keep going until you have about 10 layers, and all the vegetables and cheese are used up. Finish with a layer of dough, pressing down on it to flatten it a little, and spread with last of the butter. Refrigerate for 2 hours or up to 5 days.

Preheat the oven to 400 degrees F. Bake the lasagna for about 20 minutes, or until golden brown. Serve with your favorite red sauce.

Makes 8 to 10 servings

MOUNT RAINIER NATIONAL PARK

*...the most extravagantly beautiful of all the alpine gardens
I ever beheld in all my mountain-top wanderings.*

— JOHN MUIR
writing about Paradise Valley in 1888

MOUNT RAINIER NATIONAL PARK is located on the west side of the Cascade Range about fifty miles southeast of Seattle. The park's 235,625 acres encompasses glaciers, old-growth forests, sub-alpine meadows, and snow-topped mountains, including Mount Rainier, an active volcano that last erupted approximately a century and a half ago. Though this volcano sleeps in snow and ice, the U.S. Geological Service still considers it to be the most dangerous in the United States.

At over fourteen thousand feet, nearly three miles higher than the valleys to the west, Mount Rainier dominates the skyline of western Washington. Its familiar silhouette has captured human imagination since prehistoric times. Native people called it Takhoma, or "big mountain." Captain George Vancouver named it Mount Rainier while exploring Puget Sound in 1792.

In 1888, explorer and guide James Longmire established a camp near hot springs on Mount Rainier's shoulder and began promoting them as "healing baths." Increasing numbers of hikers, skiers, and climbers were drawn to Mount Rainier's slopes, and on March 2, 1899, Mount Rainier National Park was created.

The first access road to Paradise Valley opened in 1911, but sections were considered so dangerous that "boys under 21 and women" were prohibited from driving them. In 1912, President Taft's car bogged down in the mud and had to be pulled out by a team of mules.

PARADISE INN
A Classic Mountain Lodge

One early visitor to Mount Rainier was Stephen Mather, who climbed its summit in 1905 on a Sierra Club outing. Ten years later, as the first director of the National Park Service, he returned, hoping to fund a lodge suitable to the setting. At Mount Rainier, as in other parks, early development was haphazard. Greater unity and better design of park facilities were high priorities for the newly formed park service. At Zion, Grand Canyon, and elsewhere, Mather had tapped railroad companies for investment in park lodging. But since trains couldn't climb Mount Rainier, Mather had to find other resources to construct a lodge on its slopes.

He invited a group of Seattle and Tacoma businessmen for a tour of the peak, and then told his guests that if they didn't form a local company to build a lodge, he would bring in eastern capital to do the job. In 1916, local business leaders formed the Rainier National Park Company (RNPC).

RNPC investors hiked to a promising site for the proposed lodge, a grassy sub-alpine meadow overlooking Paradise Valley, with views of Mount Rainier's summit and the distant Tatoosh Range. Nearby was the Silver Forest, a stand of dead Alaska cedars burned by a fire in 1885. Over the years, the snags had weathered to a glossy silver color.

Soon after the site was selected, timbers from the Silver Forest were cut and hauled to the future site of the Paradise Inn. Stone for the foundation was quarried locally and stockpiled along with the timber to prepare for the short building season. RNPC hired Tacoma architects Heath, Grove, and Bell, and work on the stone foundation began in July of 1916.

Frederick Heath's design was influenced by the work of landscape architect Frederick Law Olmsted, Jr. Form and materials tied the inn to the landscape. The design offered the rustic but cohesive image that Stephen Mather was seeking: a shingled roof, steeply pitched to withstand heavy snows, with gables and dormers that brought nature indoors with a changing play of light and shadow.

When the Paradise Inn opened a year later, on July 1, 1917, the road was still blocked with snow. Visitors took sleighs or horses

Opposite: James Longmire first brought attention to Mount Rainier touting the hot springs as "healing baths."
Below: A unique feature of the inn is the use of timbers from the nearby Silver Forest, which was a stand of dead Alaska cedars.

The posts in the dining room are painted in Swiss floral designs.

up Paradise Valley to the inn. Waterproof boots were offered to guests who wanted to hike the rest of the way.

On arrival, guests stepped into one of the inn's most impressive spaces, the lobby "forested" with the silvery Alaska cedar logs, which acted as structural framework. Enormous stone fireplaces anchored the north and south ends of the room, capable of burning a cord of wood a day.

Woodwork, including the detailing of the registration area, was completed by German carpenter Hans Fraehnke over the winter. He also handcrafted several furniture pieces—including a grandfather clock, piano, tables, and benches—that season the

alpine ambience with a touch of Bavarian whimsy. The piano, played by President Harry Truman during his visit, was detailed with heavy log corner posts of peeled logs with whittled ends.

The original building included the lobby, dining room, and kitchen wings to the north. The inn's thirty-seven guestrooms were located on the second floor above the dining room and in the three-story east wing. In 1920, a four-story annex designed by RNPC architect Harlan Thomas added a hundred new guestrooms for the growing number of visitors.

The inn's dining room is nearly as impressive as the lobby, with an exposed structural system and posts painted in Swiss

Not long after the Olympic trials, the inn opened for its first full winter season, and a portable ski tow was installed.

The Paradise slopes were busy again in the winter of 1941, when park rangers assisted two U.S. Army ski patrol detachments, the 15th Infantry and the 41st Division, in wartime training. The following winter, five hundred infantrymen from the 87th Mountain Infantry Regiment were stationed at Paradise. Despite the wartime focus, public skiing continued. Soldiers helped sponsor ski events, setting courses, furnishing doctors for first aid, and operating radios for weekend contests.

In 1952, RNPC sold the Paradise Inn to the National Park Service, which in turn leased it to concessionaires. The inn continued to undergo additions and updates, though the historic character of the lobby and dining room has been maintained. In 1997, the Paradise Inn and surrounding buildings were designated a National Historic Landmark District, showcasing the rustic-style architecture of the twenties and thirties.

Left: The mountain was host to athletes competing in the 1934-35 U.S. Olympic trials.

floral designs. Chandeliers are made of logs with wrought iron detailing. Walls are of dark wood wainscoting. A stone fireplace and chimney at the north end lend a warm atmosphere.

The inn has welcomed various movie stars and dignitaries, including Sonja Henie, Shirley Temple, Tyrone Power, Frances Farmer, Cecil B. DeMille, the crown prince of Norway, and President Harry Truman.

In 1934-35, Paradise hosted athletes competing in the U.S. Olympic trials and national skiing championship. German skier Hans Schroll, whose yodeling delighted the crowds, won the men's downhill nearly two minutes ahead of the second-place finisher. Sportscasters broadcast the events to households across the nation. Three wire services covered details for the newspapers; moviegoers watched Paramount newsreels of the action.

IMPROVING ON PARADISE

Mount Rainier is the highest and snowiest peak in the Cascade Range, with an annual average snowfall of more than six hundred inches. Almost two-thirds of the way down the mountain, at five thousand feet, snow depth may reach fifteen to twenty feet. Paradise is, according to experts, the snowiest place on earth, with some winters bringing more than a thousand inches of snow.

Little wonder that the Paradise Inn has required constant maintenance and multiple structural upgrades. The inn's structural system of posts, beams, and trusses is augmented by a system of cables and steel. The entry bays are supported by steel T-beams hidden inside hollowed logs. Dining room posts are wrapped with cable below the diagonal bracing to keep the posts from cracking and splitting under the weight of snow.

In one of the largest construction projects ever undertaken by the National Park Service, the Paradise Inn and visitor center are being overhauled as part of a two-year, thirty-million-dollar project. For the first time since it opened in 1917, the inn will be closed, with the grand reopening slated for the year 2008. Plans include restoring the building to its original condition, reversing a 1970s remodel.

BOURBON BUFFALO MEATLOAF

3 tablespoons butter

1 cup minced onion

1 cup minced celery

2 cloves garlic, minced

2 pounds ground buffalo meat

1 tablespoon Worcestershire sauce

2 eggs

1 cup ketchup

Dash of Tabasco

½ teaspoon ground cumin

1 teaspoon salt

½ teaspoon pepper

1 tablespoon chopped fresh parsley

2 tablespoons lemon juice

Preheat the oven to 350 degrees F. Melt the butter in a heavy skillet. Add the onions, celery, and garlic, cooking until soft but not browned. Transfer the vegetables to a large mixing bowl and add the meat, Worcestershire sauce, eggs, ½ cup of the ketchup, Tabasco, cumin, salt, pepper, parsley, and lemon juice. Mix thoroughly with damp hands.

Pat the meat mixture into a buttered baking dish. Bake for 35 minutes. Remove from oven to cover the top of the loaf with the remaining ketchup. Return to oven and bake until done, about 10 more minutes. Serve with Jack Daniel's Sauce.

Makes 8 servings

JACK DANIEL'S SAUCE

1 tablespoon olive oil

1 tablespoon chopped shallots

1 tablespoon minced garlic

1 cup Jack Daniel's Tennessee Whiskey

1 bay leaf

1 sprig thyme

1 quart demi-glace
(gravy or thickened stock can be substituted)

1 cup barbecue sauce

Salt and pepper

Heat the oil in a skillet over medium heat. Sauté the shallots and garlic. Deglaze the pan with the whiskey. Add bay leaf and thyme. Cook until the liquid is reduced by half. Add demi-glace and barbecue sauce. Simmer for 15 minutes or until the sauce reaches desired consistency. Season to taste with salt and pepper. Serve warm.

Makes 5 cups

YAKAMA SPINACH SALAD

1 ½ pounds spinach leaves

1 Granny Smith apple, sliced

4 ounces Gorgonzola cheese, crumbled

8 ounces candied walnuts

2 cups Pear Vinaigrette or
Pear and Cranberry Dressing

Divide the spinach among four chilled plates. Top each salad with five slices of apple. Sprinkle salads evenly with Gorgonzola cheese and top with candied walnuts. Serve with Pear Vinaigrette (page 119) or Pear and Cranberry Dressing (page 119).

Makes 4 servings

CANDIED WALNUTS

Nonstick vegetable oil spray

6 tablespoons plus 3 tablespoons sugar

2 tablespoons orange juice

2 cups walnut halves

½ teaspoon ground cinnamon

Preheat the oven to 375 degrees F. Line a large cookie pan with foil, and spray the foil with nonstick spray. Mix the 6 tablespoons of sugar with orange juice in a 10-inch skillet over medium heat. Bring to a simmer, and then add the walnuts. Cook, stirring constantly, until liquid is absorbed and mixture starts to caramelize. Remove from heat.

Combine the cinnamon and the remaining 3 tablespoons of sugar in a small bowl. Toss the walnuts in the cinnamon mixture until coated. Arrange them in a single layer on the cookie pan. Bake until the walnuts appear crystallized and toasted. Let them cool before using in recipes or serving as a snack.

Makes 2 cups

PEAR AND CRANBERRY DRESSING

½ cup canned pears with juice

1 cup cranberry sauce

¼ cup Riesling wine

Place the pears and juice, cranberry sauce, and Riesling in a food processor or blender. Process on high for 2 minutes, adding additional pear juice if the mixture is too thick. Chill before using.

Makes 2 cups

PEAR VINAIGRETTE

1 Bartlett pear, cored and coarsely chopped

1 tablespoon grated white or yellow onion

¼ cup honey

½ teaspoon kosher or sea salt

½ cup apple cider vinegar

1 teaspoon Dijon mustard

¼ teaspoon Tabasco

2 tablespoons hazelnut or walnut oil

3 tablespoons canola oil

In a blender or food processor, pulse the pear, onion, honey, salt, vinegar, mustard, and Tabasco. Add the hazelnut and canola oils. Pulse until the mixture thickens slightly. Cover and refrigerate for up to one week.

Makes 1⅔ cups

STUFFED PORTOBELLO MUSHROOMS

4 portobello mushrooms

8 ounces mozzarella, provolone,
and Parmesan cheeses, shredded

1 cup breadcrumbs

1 teaspoon chopped garlic

2 tablespoons chopped yellow onion

1 cup shredded spinach leaves

2 tablespoons olive oil

1 teaspoon seasoning mix
(thyme, basil, pepper, and oregano)

Fresh basil for garnish

Preheat grill. (Alternatively, preheat oven to 475 degrees F.) Remove the stems from the mushrooms, and set the caps aside. Dice the stems and place them in a large bowl. Add cheeses, breadcrumbs, garlic, onion, spinach, olive oil, and seasoning. Mix thoroughly.

Clean the gills of the mushrooms. Using a paring knife, score the caps and rub them with olive oil. Grill the mushroom caps for 2 to 3 minutes (or place on a sheet pan and heat them in the oven).

Preheat (or turn down) oven to 350 degrees F. Fill each cap with one-fourth of the stuffing mixture and press down firmly. Arrange on a sheet pan and bake for 25 minutes. Garnish with fresh basil before serving.

Makes 4 servings

LONGMIRE SANDWICH

2 zucchinis

2 yellow crookneck squashes

2 green bell peppers

2 red bell peppers

6 mushrooms

1 eggplant

8 slices Swiss cheese

2 hoagie rolls

Preheat grill or prepare a sauté pan. Slice zucchinis lengthwise, making 8 slices. Slice the yellow squashes lengthwise into 8 slices. Cut the red and green peppers into julienne pieces. Slice the mushrooms. Peel and slice the eggplant.

Grill or sauté the squash slices and set aside. Grill or sauté the peppers and mushrooms and set aside. Grill or sauté the eggplant and set aside.

Preheat oven broiler. Slice the hoagie rolls in half and arrange on a sheet pan. Layer each half with 2 slices of zucchini, 2 slices of yellow squash, and equal amounts of peppers, mushrooms, and eggplant. Top each sandwich with 2 slices of cheese. Place under the broiler until the cheese is melted. Serve with chips.

Makes 4 servings

ORANGE-CRANBERRY HALIBUT

1 cup orange juice

1 cup cranberry juice

½ cup cran-raisins

1 tablespoon hoisin sauce

1 tablespoon honey

½ teaspoon arrowroot

4 halibut fillets, about 7 ounces each

Orange twists for garnish

Place orange juice, cranberry juice, cran-raisins, hoisin sauce, and honey in a small saucepan and heat until just boiling. Mix arrowroot with a little water and pour into the sauce, stirring, until thickened. Turn off heat, and cover the pan to keep sauce warm.

Preheat grill. Grill halibut about 3 minutes per side, or until done. Arrange fillets on a platter or on individual plates. Spoon warm sauce over the top and garnish with orange twists. Serve immediately.

Makes 4 servings

ORANGE PECAN TROUT

2 cups orange juice

Zest of one orange

2 tablespoons tarragon

4 boneless trout fillets

2 cups panko (Japanese breadcrumbs)

½ cup chopped pecans

½ cup (1 stick) butter

Orange twists for garnish

Place the orange juice in a glass baking dish and add orange zest and tarragon. Place the trout in the orange marinade and chill for at least two hours. Mix the panko and pecans in a shallow dish. Melt the butter in a large sauté pan over medium heat. Remove the trout from the marinade. Press each fillet into the crumb mixture, skin side up, making sure that the fillets are coated with crumbs. Place the fillets, skin side up, in the sauté pan and cook until golden brown, about 6 minutes. Turn over the fillets and cook an additional 3 to 5 minutes, until done. Garnish with an orange twist and serve with rice and vegetables.

Makes 4 servings

FRUIT OF THE FOREST PORK LOIN

Pork loin, about 5 pounds

Salt and pepper

Chopped garlic

12 slices toasted wheat bread

2 cups chopped cran-raisins

1 cup pine nuts

1 Granny Smith apple, diced

1 cup orange juice

2 teaspoons dried sage

2 teaspoons rosemary

1 teaspoon cinnamon

Preheat oven to 350 degrees F. Rub the pork loin with salt, pepper, and garlic and roast for about 30 minutes. Meanwhile, make the stuffing. Cube the toasted bread and place in a large mixing bowl. Add cran-raisins, pine nuts, and diced apple, tossing to mix. Then stir in the orange juice, sage, rosemary, and cinnamon, seasoning with salt and pepper to taste.

Remove the pork from the oven and carve it into half-inch thick slices. Arrange the pork slices on a sheet pan. Top each slice with a spoonful of the stuffing. Place the pork back in the oven and bake and additional 15 minutes. Serve with a potato dish and a seasonal vegetable.

Makes 8 servings

BUFFALO STEW

3 pounds buffalo stew meat, cut into 1-inch chunks

2 medium yellow onions, diced

2 teaspoons cumin seed

1 cup plus 3 cups beef broth

2 tablespoons chili powder

12 medium white or Yukon Gold potatoes,
skin on, scrubbed, and cut into chunks

1 ½ pounds carrots,
cleaned and cut into inch-long sticks

2 cups fresh or frozen corn kernels

3 (7-ounce) cans whole green chiles, cut into strips

Salt

Fresh cilantro sprigs for garnish

Braise the buffalo meat in a large skillet. Add the onions, cumin, and 1 cup of the beef broth. Cover and cook on high heat for 20 minutes. Uncover and continue cooking until the broth evaporates and the meat browns. Stir in chili powder, adding enough broth to loosen browned bits from the skillet. Continue stirring until liquid evaporates. Stir in the remaining broth. Add potatoes, carrots, corn, and green chiles. Cover and simmer until tender, approximately 1 hour. Season to taste with salt. Garnish with cilantro before serving.

Makes 6 servings

MOUNT HOOD NATIONAL FOREST

Timberline Lodge was distinctly an experiment to get away from the leaf-raking type of project. It was to be a monument to the skill and industry of the unemployed and it is a monument the world will have to acknowledge.

— E. J. GRIFFITH
Oregon's WPA Administrator

J UST TWENTY MILES EAST of Portland, Oregon's Mount Hood National Forest extends south from the Columbia River Gorge for more than sixty miles, sprawling over both east and west slopes of the Cascade Range and encompassing forested mountains, lakes, and streams.

The forest's million-plus acres contain nearly two hundred thousand acres of designated wilderness. The largest is Mount Hood Wilderness, which includes the mountain's upper slopes. Mount Hood, known to area Indians as Wy'East, rises 11,237 feet above sea level. Like Mount Rainier to the north, also part of the Cascade range, Mount Hood is another "sleeping volcano." Vulcanologists predict that Mount Hood could erupt again before the end of this century.

In a Northwest Indian tale about the fiery Cascades, Mount St. Helens was once a beautiful maiden named Loowit. Two sons of the Great Spirit fell in love with her, and she could not decide between them. The brothers, Wy'East and Klickitat, hurled rocks and burned forests as they fought over her. The Great Spirit struck down the three lovers and created mountain peaks where each fell. Loowit (Mount St. Helens) is a beautiful, dazzling white. Wy'East (Mount Hood) proudly lifts his head, while Klickitat (Mount Adams) bows his head in sorrow to see Loowit encased in ice and snow.

In 1792, cartographers from the British Royal Navy were the first Europeans to see the mountain. They named it after a naval hero, Alexander Hood—a man who would never see its slopes. The first Americans to see Mount Hood, Lewis and Clark, recorded the distant sighting on November 3, 1805.

By the 1880s, many recreational climbers were taking on the slopes of Mount Hood. The Cascade Range Forest Reserve was established in 1893 and later divided into several national forests. The name was changed to Mount Hood National Forest in 1924. The varied terrain and climate zones offer a wide range of recreation opportunities, from climbing to boating to mushrooming. Twelve hundred miles of trails lead to forests, lakes, and slopes. The mountain ski resort is a favorite destination for skiers and snowboarders—a quarter of a million head for its slopes each winter.

TIMBERLINE LODGE
The Pride of a Nation

For years Portland businessman Emerson J. Griffith tried to persuade developers to build a lodge on Mount Hood. When the Great Depression hit, Griffith became the state's director for the Works Progress Administration (WPA). He immediately requested funding for a "recreation project"—the lodge he'd dreamed of—and in 1935 the WPA approved the project.

From the very beginning, Timberline Lodge was the work of many hands. In the spring of 1936, surveyors measured the site when it was buried under fourteen feet of snow. Forest service employees used heavy equipment to clear the access road so WPA workers and materials could be brought to the site. The crew needed to remove three feet of snow covering the site before the June groundbreaking.

Though the lodge's concept is usually credited to Gilbert Stanley Underwood, a group of U.S. Forest Service architects and landscape designers completed the final drawings. Architect Linn A. Forrest wrote, "The shape of the central lounge was inspired by the character and outline of the mountain peak. It was our hope not to detract from the great natural beauty of the area. The entire exterior was made to blend as nearly as possible with the mountainside."

Call it Cascadian, Neovernacular, Oregon Rustic, Stately Picturesque, or Big-Stick style; the building is based on the parkitecture model established by Underwood at Yosemite, Grand Canyon, Zion, and other national parks. It combines tradition and function while harmonizing with the natural mountainside setting. The lodge is also a showcase of handcraft, with carved and inlaid woodwork, wrought iron, weaving, applique, painting, mosaic, and stained glass.

Two wings extend from a hexagonal hub. The silver-gray exterior color, which helps the lodge blend with the rocky landscape, was created by a WPA painter. The forest service made the color standard for its construction in the Northwest: "This paint, which simulates frost, is remarkable not only for its realism, but for its economy of cost."

Regional materials were used, including fir, pine, oak, and cedar from the nearby forests, and four hundred tons of locally

The lodge offers a clear view of Mount Hood.

Interior designer Margery
Hoffman Smith thought of every
detail when designing the lodge.

quarried stone. Even the flax and wool used in upholstery, bed-spreads, and draperies were locally raised.

Underwood acted as a consultant for the decor, but Margery Hoffman Smith, a Portland interior designer working for the Federal Art Project, was Timberline's chief designer. She influenced every detail, from the rugs on the floors to the seven-hundred-pound weathervane that tops the hexagonal head house.

Smith employed twenty-three different motifs, favoring American Indian designs and local wildflowers, which were used in draperies, bedspreads, and rugs, as well as in watercolor paintings made by Karl Feuer. In true Depression-era spirit, textiles were fashioned from recycled fabrics. Old uniforms and blankets were

used for the hand-hooked rugs. (The lodge's textiles have been replaced twice with handcrafted replicas of the original designs.)

Construction continued all winter long. Snowplows kept access roads open and portable stoves were brought in to warm stonemasons' hands. A mere fifteen months later, on September 28, 1937, President Franklin D. Roosevelt dedicated Timberline Lodge, declaring it "a monument to the skill and faithful performance of workers on the rolls of the Works Progress Administration" and "a new adjunct to the national prosperity."

Tragically, the hard work and vision of those who contributed to Timberline Lodge was nearly lost through neglect, overuse, and even vandalism. Four different concessionaires failed to make

lodge as it was when it first opened. The hotel has even starred in a couple of movies, including The Shining (1980). (Who could forget that sweeping aerial shot?)

Timberline's dining room has been in a couple of productions of its own, appearing in a PBS documentary and starring in a cookbook featuring the lodge's cuisine. Executive chef Leif Benson, considered a pioneer of Pacific Northwest cuisine, has been the certified executive chef at Timberline for the past twenty-six years. Some of his latest creations include Cinnamon Granola French Toast (page 132).

Left above: The Cascadian archway leading to the lower lobby is a defining decorative element of the lodge.
Left below: The mosaic in the lower lobby features animals from the surrounding forest

THE WPA
Building America

To create desperately needed jobs during the Great Depression, President Franklin Roosevelt established several agencies, including the Works Progress Administration (WPA). Workers earned about forty-five dollars a month on public projects, such as building city sidewalks.

Ninety percent of the men and women who worked on Timberline Lodge were hired by the WPA. The project employed about a hundred construction workers at a time, but jobs were rotated in order to employ as many of the jobless as possible.

Skilled laborers were paid ninety cents per hour, others fifty-five cents. Many of the project's skilled stonemasons were Italian immigrants whose English language skills were limited, preventing them from finding employment in the private sector. Master artisans supervised and instructed junior workers so that they could learn job skills.

Construction workers lived in a tent city at Summit Meadows, about half a mile below the job site. Trucks delivered workers to the site, a rough drive that could take an hour in bad weather. Hot meals were provided three times daily. The crews worked quickly, hoping to finish as much of the outdoor work as possible before winter set in, and also because no one was sure how long the WPA could continue providing jobs in such an uncertain economy.

Timberline Lodge, a stunning example of architecture and interior design, cost less than one million dollars to build. When all WPA programs came to an end in 1943, they had cost the nation eleven million dollars. In return, these projects provided needed civic infrastructure, many cultural treasures, and a sense of worth and confidence to those devastated by the Great Depression.

the lodge a financial success. Timberline was closed during World War II and again in 1955 for unpaid electric bills.

About that time, a young veteran named Richard Kohnstamm moved to Oregon to take a job at a Portland social-service agency. Though the lodge was closed and littered with damaged artwork and mattresses, he recognized its romantic past. Kohnstamm, then twenty-nine years old, bid on the operations concession and won. Over the years the Kohnstamm family, along with the Forest Service and the nonprofit Friends of Timberline, have worked to preserve and restore the lodge and its amazing collection of regional arts and crafts.

Thanks to their efforts, today's guests can experience the

CINNAMON GRANOLA FRENCH TOAST

8 eggs, beaten

Zest from 1 orange

1 teaspoon vanilla extract

¼ cup milk

8 slices sourdough bread

Butter

4 cups granola (your favorite or Cascade Granola)

Cinnamon sugar

Whipped butter

Maple syrup

Fresh seasonal fruit, for garnish

Mix the eggs, orange zest, vanilla, and milk. Soak the bread slices in egg mixture. Heat a cast iron skillet or pancake griddle and coat it with butter. Place the soaked bread on the griddle. Sprinkle a layer of granola onto the uncooked side of the bread and press lightly with a pancake turner to make it stick. Turn the slices over when the undersides are golden brown and lightly press again.

Remove French toast from the pan when it is cooked through and golden brown. (Granola will be on only one side.) Sprinkle with cinnamon sugar and serve with whipped butter and maple syrup. Garnish with fresh seasonal fruit.

Makes 4 servings

CASCADE GRANOLA

3 cups old-fashioned rolled oats

⅓ cup slivered almonds

⅓ cup chopped walnuts

⅓ cup chopped pecans

⅓ cup grated coconut

4 ½ teaspoons cinnamon

2 ½ teaspoons cloves

1 ½ teaspoons nutmeg

⅓ cup honey

⅓ cup peanut oil

1 ½ teaspoons vanilla

2 tablespoons dark corn syrup

⅓ cup raisins

Preheat the oven to 350 degrees F. Mix the oats, nuts, coconut, cinnamon, cloves, and nutmeg in a large bowl. Combine the honey, oil, vanilla, and corn syrup in a small saucepan. Heat until mixture is not quite boiling. Mix the hot liquid with the dry ingredients, stirring thoroughly.

Pour the mixture onto a large baking pan. Bake for 30 minutes, stirring every 5 minutes. Remove from oven and stir in raisins. Cool. Store in an airtight container.

Makes 2½ quarts

WATERMELON, TOMATO, AND FETA SALAD
with White Balsamic Vinaigrette

1 gallon cubed watermelon

1 quart cubed ripe tomatoes

2 cups crumbled feta cheese

3 cups chopped fresh cilantro

1 cup olive oil

⅓ cup white balsamic vinegar

Salt and pepper

Combine the watermelon, tomatoes, cheese, and cilantro in a large bowl. Toss with the oil and vinegar. Season to taste with salt and pepper. Serve immediately.

Makes 20 servings

SMOKED GOUDA AND ARTICHOKE DIP

2 (14-ounce) cans marinated artichoke hearts, drained

1 (8-ounce) package spinach, steamed

1 pound smoked Gouda, grated

1 (8-ounce) package cream cheese

¼ pound blue cheese

Salt and pepper

Prepare a grill and preheat the oven to 350 degrees F. Roast the artichoke hearts on the grill. Chop the artichokes and combine with the spinach and cheeses in a food processor, mixing well. Spoon into in ovenproof dish.

Bake the spinach-cheese mixture until bubbling. Serve hot or chilled with pita chips or grilled flatbread.

SUMMER SQUASH PANCAKES

6 green zucchini, grated

6 yellow squash, grated

2 cups minced onion

3 eggs, beaten

1 bunch fresh dill, chopped

3 cups flour

2 tablespoons baking powder

Salt and pepper

Butter

Combine the grated squash, onion, eggs, and dill in a large bowl. Mix the flour and baking powder, seasoning with salt and pepper. Combine wet and dry ingredients, mixing lightly. Preheat a griddle or skillet and coat with melted butter. Drop dough onto hot griddle to form 3-inch pancakes. Cook both sides until golden brown. Serve with Turkish Dill Sauce.

Makes 8 to 10 servings

TURKISH DILL SAUCE

1 (32-ounce) carton yogurt

1 cup panko or very fine bread crumbs

3 teaspoons minced garlic

Juice of 1 lemon

½ bunch fresh dill

Salt and pepper

Mix the yogurt, panko, garlic, lemon juice, and dill. Season to taste with salt and pepper. Chill until serving.

MANGO SALSA

1 ½ packages frozen mango chunks, thawed

½ cup diced red onion

½ cup diced red pepper

2 serrano chiles or jalapeños, seeded and minced

1 cup chopped fresh cilantro

¼ cup lime juice

1 tablespoon rice wine vinegar

Pinch of salt

Sugar, if needed

Mix together mangoes, onion, red pepper, chiles, and cilantro. Stir in the lime juice and vinegar. Season with salt and, if needed, sugar. Refrigerate until serving.

Makes 4 servings

CHILLED ORGANIC CARROT SOUP
with Mango and Coconut

1 gallon carrot juice, preferably organic

3 (16-ounce) packages frozen mango chunks

1 cup cream of coconut

1 cup coconut milk

1 stalk fresh lemongrass, peeled and chopped

½ cup chopped fresh ginger

¼ cup lime juice

⅛ cup Thai-style sweet chili sauce

½ serrano chile, seeded and chopped

Mango Salsa, for garnish

Additional cream of coconut, for garnish

Crushed Szechuan pepper, for garnish

Combine the carrot juice, mango, cream of coconut, coconut milk, lemongrass, ginger, lime juice, chili sauce, and chile. Purée mixture in batches using a blender. Strain through a sieve.

Serve chilled. Garnish with Mango Salsa (page 137), additional coconut cream, and crushed Szechuan pepper (optional).

Makes 1½ gallons

GRAND TETON NATIONAL PARK

I defy the annals of chivalry to furnish the record of a life more wild
and perilous than that of a Rocky Mountain trapper.
— FRANCIS PARKMAN

THE TETON RANGE, A FAULT-BLOCK RANGE forty miles long, includes twelve peaks that are over twelve thousand feet. The most recognizable is Grand Teton, whose jagged silhouette rises nearly fourteen thousand feet, a landmark for travelers since prehistoric times. Located in northwestern Wyoming, Grand Teton National Park protects these mountains, nearby canyons, slopes, and valleys. Yellowstone's earliest human inhabitants were American Indians, and archaeological evidence dates their presence to thousands of years ago. The first white man to visit Yellowstone was likely John Colter, of the Lewis and Clark Expedition, who admired the West so much he stayed after other expedition members returned home in 1806. Few others were aware of the area until 1871, when Ferdinand V. Hayden, head of the U.S. Geological Survey, assembled a survey party that included photographer William H. Jackson and artist Thomas Moran. The Hayden survey confirmed rumors of this wonderland of geology and scenery and helped inspire the establishment of the national park.

Between the summit and the valley lying six thousand feet below, forests and meadows are home to black bear, elk, moose, mule deer, bison, and pronghorn. Grizzlies range throughout more remote areas, and bald eagles soar above crystal-clear alpine lakes.

Though winters were too fierce for permanent residence, the area's rich and diverse flora and fauna made it a seasonal stopping

place for humans, who started visiting the Jackson Hole area about ten thousand years ago. Bands of Paleo-Indians camped near the Tetons soon after the last major ice age ended. Modern tribes—Shoshone, Crow, Gros Ventre, and Blackfeet—also traveled through the area, as did Lewis and Clark's expedition.

Two decades later, the beaver fur trade lured trappers, hunters, and traders to the West. From about 1820 to 1840, mountain men from throughout the Rocky Mountains gathered annually to exchange furs for supplies, tobacco, liquor and news in events known as "rendezvous." They met at the distinctive Teton Range, where several trapping routes intersected, before heading on to the rendezvous site.

But the solitary—and dangerous—life of the mountain man was about to end. The Homestead Act of 1862 granted land to those who promised to build on it and live there for five years. Ranchers and farmers entered the Jackson Hole area, willing to brave the remote location and hard winters for free land and the dream of a new life.

After the devastating winter of 1886-87, when sixty to ninety-five percent of western herds perished, many ranchers gave up or hired themselves out as guides and opened their ranches to guests. Visitors had been entering the region since neighboring Yellowstone became the world's first national park. Attracting visitors to an area already known for scenery and wildlife proved to be a more reliable and profitable venture than agriculture. In 1907, homesteader Louis Joy opened the first dude ranch.

The Tetons first received government protection in 1897 with the creation of the Teton Forest Reserve. Horace Albright, assistant to Stephen Mather of the National Park Service, visited the region in 1916. Albright was impressed with the Tetons and Jackson Hole. In a report to the Secretary of the Interior, Mather and Albright stated that protecting the Tetons, Jackson Lake, and Snake River was "one of seven urgent needs facing the Park Service."

But the forest service, along with some ranchers and dude ranch operators, fought and defeated all attempts to federalize land near Jackson Hole. In 1923 park supporters outlined a new approach: wealthy individuals would buy private land, then be reimbursed by congress. Major supporter John D. Rockefeller wrote Albright in 1926: "Send me an estimate as to what it would take to buy the land and clear the junk out of this area, and send me a map."

Over a period of years, Rockefeller quietly bought up more than thirty-three thousand acres of land for less than one-and-a-half million dollars. In 1943, President Franklin Delano Roosevelt declared Jackson Hole a National Monument, but a partisan congress continued to resist efforts to create a national park. At last, after long opposition, Grand Teton National Park was created in 1950.

A refuge for many animal and plant species, the area offers humans a mixture of wilderness and recreation experiences, including mountaineering, mountain biking, horseback riding, scenic floats, whitewater rafting, fly fishing, and winter sports such as snowshoeing and skiing.

JACKSON LAKE LODGE
Ushering in a New Era

On a bluff overlooking Jackson Lake, where John D. Rocke-feller Jr. had first seen the Teton Range twenty-seven years earlier, construction of a new lodge began in 1953.

Though the former director, Horace Albright, had left the National Park Service for private industry, he recommended that Gilbert Stanley Underwood—already retired—design Jackson Lake Lodge. The lodge was a definite departure from Under-wood's rustic style, striking a compromise between the Bauhaus architecture popular at the time and the spectacular natural set-ting. As he did with The Ahwahnee, Underwood used stained concrete exteriors formed to look like wood. The lodge's inter-national design was efficient and stark, signaling a new era.

Appropriately, the lodge was the site of the 1989 talks be-tween U.S. Secretary of State James Baker and Soviet Foreign Minister Eduard Shevardnadze. Here, overlooking Jackson Lake with the Teton Range as backdrop, the two nations signed a statement of peace and friendship that helped establish the détente leading to the end of the Cold War.

Over the years, Presidents Kennedy, Nixon, Reagan, Clin-ton, and Lady Bird Johnson have all visited Jackson Lake Lodge, which recently celebrated its fiftieth anniversary.

Jackson Lake Lodge offers fine dining in the Mural Room, named for the seven-hundred-square-foot mural painted by western artist Carl Roters in 1959. The mural, which covers two walls of the dining room, depicts a mountain man rendezvous. Many mountain men left their legacy in place names, such as Davey Jackson, who trapped in the "hole"—a valley surrounded by mountains—that came to bear his name. A huge picture win-dow facing west offers dramatic views of the Teton Range.

It's a scene encased in snow and ice during the winter, when the lodge is closed, but executive chef James Wallace is on duty year-round. Even though his staff is gone, Wallace uses the time preparing for the upcoming season, hiring a staff of nearly two hundred and preparing menus.

He offers some of his favorite dishes in what he terms, "A Coffee-Table Guide to the Mural Room Galaxy," a complete menu from appetizer to dessert.

Jackson Lake and the Tetons are the specutacular backdrop for diners at the Mural Room.

DUNGENESS CRAB SUNDAE

1 tablespoon wasabi paste

1 cup cocktail sauce

1 pound crabmeat (preferably Dungeness)

½ cup diced celery

4 lemon wedges

4 sprigs Italian parsley

Mix the wasabi paste with cocktail sauce. Add enough wasabi-cocktail sauce to celery to bind mixture. Portion the celery mixture into four small sherbet dishes, shallow champagne glasses, or martini glasses.

Pick over the crabmeat, discarding shells and setting aside leg portions. Divide the crabmeat between the four dishes. Top each with a dollop of the remaining cocktail sauce. Garnish with the reserved leg portions, a wedge of lemon, and a sprig of Italian parsley. Serve chilled.

Makes 4 servings

TOMATO-ONION CHUTNEY

2 tablespoons olive oil (not extra-virgin)

4 medium yellow onions

½ tablespoon Madras curry powder

1 tablespoon whole mustard seed

½ cup sugar

¼ cup rice vinegar

4 medium tomatoes, seeded and finely diced

Heat the olive oil in skillet and sauté the diced onions until almost translucent. Add the curry powder and mustard seed and sauté a few moments to bloom the flavors. Stir in the sugar until the mixture is lightly caramelized. Deglaze with the rice vinegar and reduce to a syrupy consistency.

Add the tomatoes and sauté for 2 to 3 minutes. Don't overcook; the tomatoes are best slightly firm. Serve warm or at room temperature.

Makes 4 servings

NAPOLEAN OF ORGANIC HEIRLOOM TOMATOES
and Buffalo Mozzarella

4 medium heirloom tomatoes

½ pound buffalo mozzarella cheese ball,
the same diameter as the tomatoes

1 bunch fresh basil, cleaned and separated into leaves

¼ cup extra-virgin olive oil

¼ cup balsamic glaze*

Freshly ground black pepper

Core the tomatoes with a sharp knife. Slice the tomatoes and mozzarella balls and set aside. Stack the basil leaves and slice them as thinly as possible to make a chiffonade. Pour olive oil and balsamic glaze into two squirt bottles.

To assemble, make four stacks of alternating layers of tomato and mozzarella. Place each stack in the middle of a plate. "Paint" the plate with lines of olive oil and balsamic glaze. Garnish with basil chiffonade. Using a pepper mill, grind black pepper over the entire plate. Serve chilled.

Makes 4 servings

* *Look for balsamic glaze in your grocery's vinegar or condiment section.*

ROASTED SHALLOT RISOTTO

2 tablespoons butter

½ cup minced roasted shallots

2 tablespoons minced garlic

1 cup Arborio rice

4 to 5 cups hot vegetable stock

Melt the butter in a heavy pan. Add the shallots and garlic and cook until garlic is soft. Add the rice, stirring, until grains are coated. Stir in 1 cup of the stock. Continue to stir, periodically adding more stock, for about 15 minutes, until rice is tender and has absorbed all the liquid.

Makes 4 servings

PAN-ROASTED WILD PACIFIC SALMON

2 pounds wild Pacific salmon fillets

Kosher salt

Freshly ground black pepper

1 tablespoon vegetable oil

Fresh thyme, rosemary, or Italian parsley, for garnish

Season the salmon fillets with salt and pepper. Heat the oil in a large sauté pan until very hot. Arrange the salmon in the pan bone side down and sauté until browned. Turn fillets over to brown the skin side. Salmon should be cooked medium-rare for best results. (You may need to put the fillets in a medium-hot oven to finish cooking them.)

To serve on individual plates, place a portion of Roasted Shallot Risotto (page 147) in the center of each plate. Arrange the cooked salmon on top so the risotto is still visible underneath. Top with a large spoonful Tomato-Onion Chutney (page 144) so that it cascades onto the plate. Frame the chutney with some asparagus spears or other seasonal vegetable. Garnish with a sprig of fresh thyme, rosemary, or Italian parsley.

Makes 4 servings

BAILEY'S AND BLUEBERRY POT DE CRÈME
with Kahlua Crème Anglaise

CUSTARD

3 tablespoons sugar

4 yolks from large eggs

¼ cup Bailey's Irish Cream

2 cups heavy cream

1 teaspoon vanilla

¾ cup fresh blueberries

SAUCE

¼ cup Kahlua

1 whole vanilla bean

¼ cup sugar

4 yolks from large eggs

1 cup heavy cream

1 tablespoon vanilla

Preheat the oven to 375 degrees F. To make the custard, cream together sugar and egg yolks in a stainless steel mixing bowl.

Heat the Bailey's Irish Cream in a medium saucepan until it is slightly reduced and all of the alcohol is burned off. Add the cream and vanilla. Bring the liquid to a quick boil. Remove from heat.

Add the cream mixture to the egg mixture little by little, mixing thoroughly after each addition to insure the hot liquid does not scramble the eggs. Stir in the fresh blueberries.

Select four ovenproof custard cups and fill them with the custard mixture. Place the filled cups into a baking pan with high sides. Pull out an oven rack and set the pan on it. Carefully pour hot water into the pan to a depth of ¾ inch. Gently slide the rack back into the oven. Bake about one hour, or until custard is firm.

To make the sauce, heat the Kahlua in a medium saucepan until it is slightly reduced and all the alcohol is burned off. Turn off heat. Split one whole vanilla bean and add it to the Kahlua.

Cream together the sugar and egg yolks in a stainless steel mixing bowl. Mix in cream until sugar is dissolved and mixture is smooth. Add the egg mixture to the Kahlua and slowly bring this mixture to a simmer, stirring constantly. Do not boil. As the egg yolks cook, the mixture will thicken.

Use an attractive pitcher or gravy boat to serve the sauce alongside the custards.

Makes 4 servings

GLACIER NATIONAL PARK

Old Man (Napi) came from the south, making the mountains, the prairies, and the forests as he passed along, making the birds and animals also. He traveled northward making things as he went, putting red paint in the ground here and there—arranging the world as we see it today.

— BLACKFEET CREATION LEGEND

SOMETIMES CALLED THE "backbone of the world," Glacier National Park preserves a million acres of forests, meadows, glaciers, and lakes set in the quintessential mountain scenery of the northern Rockies. Twenty thousand years ago, enormous glaciers thousands of feet thick buried the region, grinding the valleys and peaks into their present forms.

Today, seven hundred miles of hiking trails lead into a vast ecosystem that crosses the continental divide, two nations, and many traditional tribal boundaries. Mountains and plains echo with the stories of the Indians who traveled, hunted, and battled here. They considered the mountains to be spirit places with powerful medicine, leaving behind vision quest sites and other signs of their passing.

At Glacier, as in so many of the nation's parks, open tracts of lands were available because they had recently been ceded—not necessarily willingly—by Indian tribes. With the killing of the last bison in the area in 1882, starvation plagued the Blackfeet Reservation. The U.S. government acquired land from Blackfeet for one-and-a-half million dollars, opening the area to prospectors, who found copper ore deposits in the 1890s.

Supporters for national park status began to lobby congress. Among them was George Grinnell, editor of *Forest and Stream*, who had used his influence to increase aid to the Blackfeet and visited their Rocky Mountain homeland many times before the 1900s.

Lake McDonald in the winter. It is the largest lake in the park.

In 1912, Hill secured GNR's right to purchase a parcel of land from the Piegan, a Blackfeet tribe, just outside the park. Here he would build a depot and the railroad's first lodge. Inspired by the Oregon Forestry Building, which he'd seen at the 1905 Lewis and Clark Exposition in Portland, he forwarded plans and photos to architect Samuel L. Bartlett.

Bartlett and another architect, Thomas McMahon, created a lodge with Swiss chalet styling in a scale that suited the West. Hill's dream included other hotels and chalets, linked by a vast system of hiking and horseback trails, a model based on the European Alps. His broad vision gave unity and theme to a seemingly unscalable region.

Hill launched an ad campaign focused on Glacier National Park, calling it "America's Alps" and directed well-heeled visitors accustomed to European tours to "See America First." He hired artists, filmmakers, and photographers and sent them to Glacier to capture its beauty. Many photographs feature Blackfeet Indians in traditional dress, hauntingly beautiful portraits that on the one hand could be considered exploitative but on the other led to much-needed employment for the Blackfeet people.

The resulting exhibit of paintings, photographs, and film traveled the country by train, bringing the park to the people. At every stop, when the exhibit train pulled out of the depot, it left behind calendars, playing cards, posters, and other items to keep the image of the park in people's minds.

Hill hired Blackfeet Indians to ride the train and attend special events. Blackfeet tribal members also filled many positions at the new hotel, greeting visitors, participating in evening programs, preparing food, and even operating the telephone switchboard. The Blackfeet culture continues to be an important part of any visitor's Glacier National Park experience.

Despite his tireless promotional efforts and long association with the park, Hill was never commemorated by a place name, as were George Grinnell and other explorers and supporters. Hill was, however, recognized by the Blackfeet, who adopted him into the tribe and gave him the name Gray Horse Rider.

Lobbyists also included James J. Hill and his son Louis. Hill's Great Northern Railway (GNR) ran along the southern edge of the Blackfeet land. Railroad baron Hill viewed the GNR as a freight line, but his son Louis saw the potential to increase passenger travel, something other railways had accomplished at Yellowstone and Grand Canyon.

As a young man, Louis had camped and hunted in the northern Rockies, befriending local Indians and developing a love for the lakes and peaks. When he became company president in 1907, it was an opportunity to make his mark with a project completely his own.

Lobbying efforts paid off on May 11, 1910, when President Taft signed the bill creating Glacier National Park, setting aside sixteen hundred square miles of land. A year later, Louis Hill stepped down as GNR president to devote himself to his dream project of promoting and developing Glacier National Park.

GLACIER PARK LODGE
A Temple to Trees

Construction began on Glacier Park Lodge in the spring of 1912. The hotel celebrated its grand opening fifteen months later, on June 15, 1913, in conjunction with James J. Hill's seventy-fifth birthday. Six hundred invitations were mailed. When visitors stepped off the train at Glacier Park Station, they looked up to see the lodge, its mountain backdrop, and a lawn scattered with tipis and flower gardens. A thousand-foot-long, flower-lined pathway led to the great hall, where the birthday lunch was served.

The hall at Glacier Park Lodge is one of the most impressive interiors in the national parks. When workers unloaded the hall's large timbers from a freight car, the Blackfeet dubbed the new hotel "ohm-coo-mush-tah" or Big Tree Lodge.

The rectangular hall is twenty thousand square feet, with a colonnade of massive Douglas-firs that are forty-eight feet high. Each fifteen-ton log, bark intact, is crowned with a smaller horizontal log to create an Ionic capital. The log columns were brought in by rail from the Pacific northwest as trees in Montana do not typically grow to this extreme height. Light enters the temple-like space through three atriums, which are surrounded by the log columns and cross the sixty-foot roof.

The hall's original décor had an international theme, with Japanese lanterns and a staff dressed in lederhosen and kimonos, a nod to the Great Northern's Oriental Limited line to Seattle. Today the emphasis is on the lodge's native art.

The building's exterior is chalet-style, with shingled hip roofs and projecting balconies with jig-sawn railings and jerkin-head caps. Almost as soon as the hotel was completed, Hill called for a four-story annex. Connected by a breezeway to the original building, it added more than a hundred rooms and another light-filled space where guests gathered. With the addition, the tab for Glacier Park Lodge ran to half of a million dollars, not counting the three hundred thousand Hill spent on promotion in that first year alone. Things were off to an expensive, yet fantastic, start.

And Louis Hill had only just begun.

In 1927, a nine-hole golf course was built on site. This golf course was the first ever to appear in the state of Montana.

The chalet-style lodge took fifteen months to build.

153

MANY GLACIER HOTEL
Where Trails Meet

Louis Hill's next grand hotel was fifty miles from East Glacier Depot on the shore of Swiftcurrent Lake, surrounded by peaks, ridges, and glacier-carved valleys. Visitors arrived by boat, on horse or mule, or on foot. The park's largest network of trails meets here at Many Glacier Valley.

Construction began in September of 1914 on a site located below one of the area's largest glaciers. Getting materials to the site required a five-day wagon trip over primitive roads. Huge timbers for the hall were floated across Swiftcurrent and Josephine lakes and erected by Great Northern's bridge builders. The surrounding forest provided interior timbers, which were processed at a sawmill and drying kiln on site. Stone for the first floor was quarried nearby.

Two architects vied for its design; Thomas McMahon, who'd designed Glacier Park Lodge; and Kirtland Cutter, who'd been hired by another hotelier to build Lake McDonald Lodge in West Glacier. McMahon got the commission, though Cutter's influence is visible in the stone ground floor, arched windows, and gabled roof.

McMahon created a series of three four-story chalets along the lakeshore with balconies, dormers, and cupolas. With later additions, the complex was nine hundred feet long. A crew of two hundred worked all winter for the hotel to open on Independence Day 1915. The crew expanded to four hundred to complete the hotel's support buildings that summer. Although grand in scale, the hotel does not compete for attention with the surrounding peaks.

The lobby at Many Glacier Hotel is a half-size replica of the grand hall at Glacier Park Lodge. One wall bears a mural painted by Chief Medicine Owl and other chiefs, telling the history of the Blackfeet Nation. Game trophies, totem poles, and a fountain shaped like a small mountain create an outdoorsy atmosphere.

A breezeway leads to the Ptarmigan Dining Room, with its huge stone fireplace and floor-to-ceiling windows. The dining room staff dress in lederhosen or dirndls and aprons. In later years, staff members began to entertain guests with skits and musical performances, now a beloved hotel tradition.

Although grand in scale, the hotel does not compete with the surrounding peaks.

LAKE MCDONALD LODGE
Showplace on a Budget

The area's oldest hotel was built in 1895 near Apgar on the western side of the park. Little more than a fishing camp on the shores of Lake McDonald, the Snyder Hotel was purchased by a land speculator named John Lewis. Nearly eleven miles long and five hundred feet deep, Lake McDonald, known to the Kootenai as Sacred Dancing Lake, is the largest in the park.

Lewis had the old hotel removed, making way for a new lodge designed by well-connected Spokane architect Kirtland Kelsey Cutter, who had trained in New York and Europe. He was familiar with the chalet style and had experience incorporating rustic local materials, having designed an Adirondack camp for the Carnegie family.

Work on the then-named Lewis Glacier Hotel began in 1913. Building materials were floated across Lake McDonald. When the lake froze during the bitter winter months, materials were skidded across the ice. The hotel opened in June of 1914, less than a year later. In sharp contrast to the extravagant expenditures of Louis Hill, it cost a mere forty-eight thousand dollars.

Visitors arrived by train, took a coach to the lake, then crossed the lake by steamboat to the sixty-five-room lodge. They stepped off the docks and into the lodge's three-story main lobby of rough-hewn roof trusses and open balconies. Lewis, a furrier, furnished the interior with hunting trophies and pelts. The floors were of concrete shaped to look like flagstone and carved with welcoming messages in Blackfeet, Chippewa, and Cree.

The lobby was also a showcase for western art. Some say that Charles Russell inspired the designs inscribed onto the hearth of the huge inglenook fireplace. Paintings by Frank Leonard Stick, John Fery, and Gray Bartlett were among Lewis's collection.

The one-and-a-half story dining room has a rustic ambience created by exposed log walls, posts, corbels, and beams. Repairs after the 1964 flood revealed that the dining room's foundation differed from that of the rest of the lodge and may predate it.

John Lewis and Louis Hill (who had wanted to build his own hotel on Lake McDonald) developed an intense rivalry over the years. Eventually, Hill's Glacier Park Hotel Company ended up with control of the lodge, renamed Lake McDonald Hotel

During construction of the lodge, building materials were floated across the lake. When the lake froze during the winter, they were skidded across the ice.

The one-and-a-half story dining room was constructed with exposed posts and beams.

to build. The road bisected the park, climbing up and over the continental divide, passing near the Lake McDonald Hotel, and rendering long journeys via Hill's railway, steamboats, and stages unnecessary.

Harsh conditions also took a toll on the lodges and chalets that Hill had built—heavy winter snowfalls, icy cold winds, spring floods, and even avalanches. In 1936, employees at Many Glacier Hotel fought off a wildfire and saved the hotel. The response from company executives was lukewarm; they'd already begun to view Glacier Park buildings as a money pit.

Louis Hill died in 1948. By 1951, only two percent of Glacier visitors arrived by train. The Glacier hotels were given a half-hearted update (Many Glacier's "improvements" included acoustic ceiling tile and vinyl flooring over the original hardwood) to ready them for sale.

In 1987, Many Glacier Hotel was named a National Historic Landmark. Less than ten years later, the National Trust for Historic Preservation listed it with the nation's eleven "most endangered places." Basic rehabilitation was estimated at thirty million dollars.

Though not all the West's great park lodges are in such dire straits, tight budgets, changing priorities, and time itself have taken a toll on many of these landmarks. Several lodges have undergone extensive renovations in the last decade. Fortunately, the trend seems to be restoring the lodges in such ways as to honor their original aesthetics.

Several of the lessees operating the lodges today have undertaken their management with a sincere sense of stewardship, not only for the buildings themselves, but also in the greater context of being environmental stewards. At Yellowstone, Yosemite, and other national parks, chefs implement guidelines focused on using organic ingredients and ethically harvested fish, support local growers, and serve "slow food" that feeds not just the stomach but also the spirit.

(and later, Lake McDonald Lodge), after Lewis reluctantly sold it to the National Park Service in 1930.

Sadly, by the time Louis Hill gained Lake McDonald Hotel in 1930, his brilliant dream was beginning to tarnish. The stock market crash of 1929 diminished the ranks of wealthy travelers, Hill's target market. No longer could people take the sorts of vacations Hill had envisioned, twenty- or thirty-day excursions riding horseback between well-appointed resort hotels. Trailside chalets fell into disrepair, as did the hotels themselves.

Through the Great Depression and World War II, travel declined. Those who did travel chose a new means—the automobile. The Going-to-the-Sun Highway officially opened in July of 1933, an engineering marvel that cost three million dollars

THE PRINCE OF WALES HOTEL
Neighborly Hospitality

The Prince of Wales Hotel stands high on a bluff overlooking Upper Waterton Lake, its soaring roofs and Queen Anne turret a striking landmark. The hotel is the only one of Canada's grand railway hotels built by a U.S. railroad.

Louis Hill of the Great Northern Railway toured this site near the international border in 1913. Thirteen years later, construction began on architect Thomas D. McMahon's design, a seven-story building in Swiss chalet-style, with a steep, gabled roof. The GNR hoped this elegant hotel, beyond the reach of U.S. prohibition-era laws, would appeal to American tourists. The Prince of Wales Hotel opened in July of 1927.

The hotel was named for the popular Prince of Wales, who later ascended to Britain's throne as King George VIII until abdicating in 1936 to marry the woman he loved. The hotel is as wildly romantic as its namesake, with huge picture windows looking out a seven-mile-long chain of mountain peaks.

Canada created Waterton Lakes National Park in 1895, fifteen years before the U.S. set aside Glacier National Park. Because the parks are unified by nature, the U.S. congress and Canadian Parliament established them as the first International Peace Park in 1932. In 1976, the United Nations named the Waterton-Glacier International Peace Park as a World Biosphere Reserve.

The hotel appears to rule over the landscape, perched atop a high bluff.

SALMON TWO MEDICINE

GLACIER PARK LODGE

1 (8-ounce) salmon fillet

Olive oil

3 lemon wedges

2 sprigs fresh dill

PESTO

Approximately 25 fresh basil leaves

½ cup olive oil

⅓ cup pine nuts

1 cup grated Parmesan

Salt and pepper

LEMON CAPER CREAM SAUCE

¼ cup (½ stick) butter

¼ cup all purpose flour

2 ¼ cups milk

1 tablespoon very finely chopped lemon zest

1 teaspoon capers

Salt and pepper

For the pesto, combine the basil, pine nuts, and oil in a food processor. Purée. Add Parmesan and process briefly. Season to taste with salt and pepper. Set aside.

To make the sauce, melt the butter in skillet. Stir in the flour. Slowly pour in the milk, whisking constantly, until mixture begins to boil. Stir in the lemon zest and capers. Reduce heat to low, cover, and cook for 20 minutes, stirring occasionally. Season to taste with salt and pepper. Keep warm until serving.

Prepare a grill. Rub the fillet with oil and grill for approximately 3 minutes per side. Top half of the salmon with Pesto and the other half with Lemon Caper Cream Sauce. Garnish with lemon wedges and dill. Serve with wild rice pilaf and steamed broccoli.

Makes 2 servings

MONTANA BANANA SPLIT

GLACIER PARK LODGE

1 medium ripe banana, unpeeled

Nonstick cooking spray

Whipped cream

Chocolate sauce

Caramel sauce

Fruit sauce (any will do—different colors are the best)

Chopped nuts (walnuts, pecans, and peanuts)

3 large scoops ice cream
(huckleberry, chocolate, and vanilla)

Preheat oven to 350 degrees F. Coat the banana with nonstick spray or vegetable oil. Place it on a sheet pan and bake for 5 minutes. Turn the banana over and bake another 5 minutes, until the peel is dark brown to black. Remove the banana from the oven and let it cool for 10 minutes without removing the peel.

Cut through the peel, starting about an inch from one end of the banana and stopping an inch from the other end. Place it on a serving plate and push the ends toward each other to form an opening in the middle. Load the opening with the ice cream.

Top as you wish with the assorted toppings—use your imagination!

Makes 1 serving

CINNAMON-DUSTED PORK TENDERLOIN
with Raspberry Balsamic Sauce

MANY GLACIER HOTEL

1 pork tenderloin

⅓ cup ground cinnamon

3 tablespoons olive oil

1 shallot, finely chopped

2 tablespoons balsamic vinegar

⅓ cup raspberry preserves

1 tablespoon Cholula Hot Sauce

Rub the pork with cinnamon until it is completely covered. Set aside. Heat half of the oil in a small pan and sauté the shallot for 3 minutes. Add the vinegar, reduce heat, and simmer for an additional 3 minutes. Add the preserves and hot sauce and simmer for 3 minutes longer.

Preheat the oven to 350 degrees F. Heat the remaining half of the oil in an ovenproof pan. Brown the tenderloin on all sides. Roast for approximately 25 minutes, or until internal temperature reaches 165 degrees F. Let the tenderloin rest for 5 minutes.

Cut the tenderloin into 1-inch slices. Garnish with sauce. Serve with polenta and roasted baby carrots.

Makes 4 servings

BISON MEATLOAF

LAKE MCDONALD LODGE

2 bulbs garlic

1 plus 3 tablespoons balsamic vinegar

1 plus 2 tablespoons olive oil

2 sprigs fresh rosemary

1 large onion, finely chopped

2 medium green bell peppers, finely chopped

2 medium red bell peppers, finely chopped

2 pounds ground buffalo

1 pound ground beef

3 eggs

2 cups bread crumbs

2 tablespoon Cholula Hot Sauce

1 ½ to 2 cups ketchup

2 tablespoons chopped fresh sage

2 tablespoons chopped fresh thyme

2 tablespoons coarsely ground black pepper

2 tablespoons kosher salt

Mushroom Sauce

Preheat oven to 350 degrees F. Remove about a half-inch from the narrow ends of the garlic bulbs, exposing the tops of the cloves. Make a few crisscross shallow cuts through the exposed cloves. Place each head of garlic on a sheet of baking foil and drizzle with 1 tablespoon of the vinegar and 1 tablespoon of the olive oil.

Remove leaves from the rosemary sprigs and coarsely chop the stems. Chop the leaves and set aside. Scatter the stems over the garlic. Tightly wrap the foil over the garlic and bake the foil packets for 30 minutes, or until garlic is soft. Remove the garlic from the foil and cool for 20 minutes. Squeeze out the garlic pulp.

Sauté onions and peppers in the remaining 2 tablespoons of olive oil for 5 minutes. Add the remaining 3 tablespoons of vinegar, remove from heat, and let stand for 5 minutes.

Combine the roasted garlic pulp, sautéed vegetables, ground buffalo, beef, eggs, crumbs, hot sauce, ketchup, sage, thyme, reserved rosemary leaves, salt, and pepper in large bowl. Mix thoroughly. Cover and chill for 30 minutes.

Preheat oven to 350 degrees F. Press mixture into a loaf pan. Place the pan on a baking sheet. Bake until internal temperature reaches 165 degrees F. Remove and let stand for 10 minutes.

Invert pan to release loaf. Serve on a platter with Mushroom Sauce (page 163), roasted asparagus, and roasted new potatoes.

Makes 10 servings.

LINGUINI VONGOLE

1 tablespoon olive oil

⅓ of a red bell pepper, thinly sliced

2 cloves garlic, chopped

½ teaspoon red pepper flakes,
more or less according to taste

7 ounces cooked linguini, rinsed and cooled

½ pound fresh clams

⅓ cup white wine

1 (3-ounce) can clams

1 cup (packed) fresh spinach leaves

1 ½ tablespoons freshly grated Parmesan cheese

Heat the oil in a large skillet. Sauté the bell pepper, garlic, and red pepper flakes for 3 minutes. Add the fresh clams and wine. Cook until the clams open. Add the canned clams and spinach. Cook for another 3 minutes. Add the linguini and toss until pasta is coated. Add butter and toss. Add cheese and toss. Serve with grilled baguette wedges.

Makes 2 servings

MUSHROOM SAUCE

2 cups chopped mushrooms (any variety)

1 tablespoon chopped rosemary

2 shallots, finely chopped

2 tablespoons olive oil

1 cup merlot

1 ½ cups beef stock

2 tablespoons cornstarch

¼ cup cold water

1 tablespoon butter

Salt and pepper

Sauté the mushrooms, rosemary, and shallots in oil over medium-high heat for 3 minutes. Add the merlot and stock, bring to a slow boil, and cook until reduced by a third.

Whisk together the cornstarch and water. Add to the sauce, whisking constantly, until it thickens. Remove from heat. Whisk in butter. Season to taste with salt and pepper.

Makes 2 cups

SALMON RUCKO

PRINCE OF WALES HOTEL

1 10-ounce salmon fillet

2 tablespoons olive oil

LEMON-THYME BUTTER

1 pound butter, softened

⅓ cup chopped parsley

1 tablespoon lemon zest

1 tablespoon chopped capers

1 tablespoon chopped thyme

RUCKO STUFFING

¼ pound chopped clams, cooked

¼ pound baby shrimp, cooked

¼ pound oysters, cooked

½ cup bread crumbs

1 egg

1 tablespoon lemon zest

1 teaspoon chopped thyme

1 teaspoon chopped sage

1 shallot, chopped

¼ cup white wine

Combine butter, parsley, lemon zest, capers, and thyme in a food processor. Mix thoroughly. Place the butter on parchment paper and roll it into a log about 1½ inches in diameter. Refrigerate for 30 minutes.

In the meantime, prepare the stuffing. Combine the clams, shrimp, oysters, bread crumbs, egg, lemon zest, thyme, and sage in a food processor. Process until thoroughly mixed. Form into small cakes, about 2 inches in diameter and ½-inch thick. Set aside.

Prepare a grill. Rub salmon with olive oil and grill to desired doneness. Cover salmon to keep it warm and moist.

Remove Lemon-Thyme Butter from the refrigerator. Heat approximately 1 tablespoon of the Lemon-Thyme Butter in a skillet. Sauté the stuffing cakes in butter for 2 minutes on each side.

Top the salmon with the stuffing cakes and garnish with a slice of the butter (about a half-inch). Serve with saffron rice pilaf and grilled asparagus.

Makes 4 to 6 servings

CHAR-GRILLED SIRLOIN
with Caramelized Onions and Blue Cheese

PRINCE OF WALES HOTEL

1 tablespoon olive oil

1 medium onion, sliced

1 garlic clove, minced

1 10-ounce beef sirloin

2 tablespoons crumbled blue cheese

Heat the oil in a small skillet. Sauté the onions until soft. Add garlic and continue to sauté until the onions turn golden brown.

Prepare a grill. Grill the sirloin to desired doneness. Top the sirloin with cheese and onions. Serve with steak fries and a garden salad.

Makes 2 servings

MOOSE DROOL BUFFALO STRIP LOIN

MANY GLACIER HOTEL

2 tablespoons olive oil

2 cloves garlic, chopped

5 button mushrooms, quartered

1 tablespoon chopped rosemary

½ cup Moose Drool (or any local brown ale)

½ cup beef stock

1 tablespoon cornstarch

¼ cup cold water

1 tablespoon chopped thyme

Salt and pepper

1 tablespoon butter

1 (10-ounce) buffalo strip loin

Heat the oil in small skillet. Sauté the garlic and mushrooms. Stir in the rosemary. Add the ale and stock. Bring to a slow boil and cook until reduced by one-third. Combine the cornstarch and water. Add the cornstarch mixture to the sauce, stirring until it thickens. Add the thyme. Season to taste with salt and pepper. Stir in the butter.

Prepare a grill and cook the strip loin to desired doneness. Let the grilled meat rest for 3 minutes. Top with the sauce and serve with mashed potatoes and steamed snow peas.

Makes 2 servings

ACKNOWLEDGEMENTS

A sincere thank you to all the chefs who shared their time and recipes. My thanks as well to the park service staffers, concessionaires, and many others who helped with this project. You made it possible for me to bring together two of my favorite things—nature and food!

PHOTO CREDITS

Food Photography by Chris Marchetti
Bancroft Library, UC Berkeley; page 25 below right
Blackley, Pat and Chuck; page 157
Gibson, Mark E.; page 155
Grand Teton Lodge Co.; page 143
Haney, Chuck; pages 153, 156
Leif, Greg, www.LiefPhotos.com; page 128
Lindahl, Larry; pages 3, 19, 21
Luong, Quang-Tuan; pages 4, 6, 16, 18, 36, 38, 46, 48, 78, 80, 96, 98, 101, 110, 112, 115, 140, 142, 150, 152, 154
MacIntosh, Doug and Jennifer; page 52
Mount Rainier Guest Services; pages 113, 114
National Park Service; pages 25 above left, 41 below right, 55
Pflughoft, Fred; page 20
Robbins, Nancy; page 53
Thalmann, Kerry; page 126
Timberline Lodge; pages 129, 130, 131 above left and below left
Walklet, Keith; pages 49, 50, 51
Xanterra; pages 7, 8, 9, 22, 23, 24, 39, 40, 41 above left, 82, 99, 100
Yosemite Concession Services; page 54

INDEX

The Ahwahnee Hotel, 49–52
apples
    Apple-Ginger Compote, 58, 59
    Roasted Granny Apple Bisque, 58
    in Yakima Spinach Salad, 118
artichokes
    Grilled Artichokes, 105
    Smoked Gouda and Artichoke Dip, 135
    White Bean-Artichoke Spread, 60
Avocado Aioli, 72

Bailey's and Blueberry Pot De Crème, 149
Banana Split, Montana, 159
basil pesto, 158
beans
    Black Bean Soup, 26
    Blue Corn Tamales, 27
    Corn and Bean Salsa, 90
    White Bean-Artichoke Spread, 60
Béchamel Sauce, 73, 74
beef
    Bison Meatloaf, 162
    Char-Grilled Sirloin with Caramelized Onions
        and Blue Cheese, 166
    Grilled Kobe Beef Tri-Tip with Upland Cress,
        62
    New York Strip Steaks with Béarnaise Sauce, 35
    Santa Fe Steak, 45
    Western Tenderloin Hash, 86
Benson, Leif, 131
Bison Meatloaf, 162
black beans. See beans
Black Bean Soup, 26
Blueberry Pot De Crème, Bailey's and, 149
Blue Corn Tamales, 27
Bourbon Buffalo Meatloaf, 116
Boysenberry Pie, 68
Braised Garlic Chicken, 92
Breaded Wild Alaska Salmon with Heirloom
    Tomato Concassé, 13
bread pudding, date-cranberry, 85
buffalo
    Bison Meatloaf, 162
    Bourbon Buffalo Meatloaf, 116
    Buffalo Stew, 125
    Moose Drool Buffalo Strip Loin, 167
    Napoleon of Organic Heirloom Tomatoes and
        Buffalo Mozzarella, 147
Butter, Lemon-Thyme, 164

Cabbage, Stir-Fried, 15
cake. See desserts
Candied Walnuts, 118
Caper Cream Sauce, Lemon and, 158
Carrot-Ginger Soup, 91
Carrot Soup, Chilled Organic, 139
Cascade Granola, 133
Chapman, Jim, 9
Char-Grilled Sirloin with Caramelized Onions
    and Blue Cheese, 166

Charred and Peppered Salmon Club, 66
Cheesecake, Key Lime Ice-Box, with
    Pistachio Crust, 71
chicken
    Braised Garlic Chicken, 92
    Kaibab Chicken, 25, 35
    Southwest Chicken Salad, 90
    Stuffed Mojave Chicken, 93
Chile-Lime Rice, 29, 31
Chile-Olive Oil, 29, 31
chiles. See peppers and chiles
Chili, White Turkey, 55, 67
Cholula Hot Sauce, 160, 162
chutneys. See salsas and sauces
Cinnamon-Dusted Pork Tenderloin, 160
Cinnamon Granola French Toast, 132
Clam Chowder, 102
corn
    Blue Corn Tamales, 27
    in Buffalo Stew, 125
    Corn and Bean Salsa, 90
    Corn and Potato Hash, 73
    Fire-Roasted Corn Salsa, 29, 30
    Lavender-Sweet Corn Custard, 62
    Sweet Corn Bisque with Linguica and
        Pumpkin Seeds, 12
Crabmeat Gyoza, 61
Crab Sundae, Dungeness, 144
Crater Lake National Park, 96–101
Crème Anglaise, Kahlua, 149
Crème Fraîche, Curry, 58, 59
Cress, Upland, with Grilled Kobe Beef Tri-Tip, 62
Crispy Cactus Appetizer, 88
Croutons, Sourdough, 57
Curry Crème Fraîche, 58, 59

Danish Dough, 87, 88
Date-Cranberry French Toast, 85
Death Valley National Park, 78–82
desserts
    Bailey's and Blueberry Pot De Crème, 149
    Boysenberry Pie, 68
    Chocolate Truffles, 95
    Kahlua Crème Anglaise, 149
    Key Lime Ice-Box Cheesecake with
        Pistachio Crust, 71
    Marionberry Crème Brûlé, 107
    Montana Banana Split, 159
    Pine Nut Pie, 77
    Strawberry-Poppy Seed Shortcake, 69
Dill Sauce, Turkish, 136
dips and spreads
    Lemon-Thyme Butter, 164
    Smoked Gouda and Artichoke Dip, 135
    Spinach Dip, 88
    White Bean-Artichoke Spread, 60
    Zesty Mayo, 94, 95
    See also salsas and sauces
Dungeness Crab Sundae, 144
Eggplant, Navajo, 42

Elk Medallions, Seared, with Madeira Sauce, 9, 15
El Tovar, 3, 19–21

Fire-Roasted Corn Salsa, 29, 30
Fiscalini Farms Cheddar Cheese Soup, 56
fish
    Breaded Wild Alaska Salmon, 13
    Charred and Peppered Salmon Club, 66
    Orange-Cranberry Halibut, 122
    Orange Pecan Trout, 123
    Pan-Roasted Wild Pacific Salmon, 148
    Pan-Seared Salmon Tostada, 21, 29
    Prickly Pear-Smoked Trout Salad, 44
    Salmon Rucko, 164
    Salmon Two Medicine, 158
    Smoked Salmon Spinach Salad, 34
    Wild Alaska Salmon Cakes, 94
    See also seafood
French Onion Soup, 104
French Toast, Cinnamon Granola, 132
French Toast, Date-Cranberry, 85
fruit
    Apple-Ginger Compote, 58, 59
    Bailey's and Blueberry Pot De Crème, 149
    Boysenberry Pie, 68
    Date-Cranberry French Toast, 85
    Grilled Pear Salad, 11
    Key Lime Ice-Box Cheesecake with
        Pistachio Crust, 71
    Marionberry Crème Brûlé, 101, 107
    Marionberry Dressing, 108
    Marionberry Syrup, 108
    Montana Banana Split, 159
    Pear and Cranberry Dressing, 118, 119
    Pear Vinaigrette, 118, 119
    Roasted Granny Apple Bisque, 58
    Strawberry-Poppy Seed Shortcake, 69
    Wassail Punch, 72
    in Yakima Spinach Salad, 118
Fruit of the Forest Pork Loin, 124
Furnace Creek Inn, 81–82

Garden Phyllo Lasagna, 109
garlic, roasted, 60
Garlic Chicken, Braised, 92
Glacier National Park, 150–57
Gouda Cream Sauce, 105
Grand Canyon National Park, 3, 16–25
Grand Marnier Whipped Cream, 69
Grand Teton National Park, 140–43
Granola, Cascade, 133
Grilled Artichokes, 105
Grilled Kobe Beef Tri-Tip with Upland Cress, 62
Grilled Pear Salad with Cambozola Cheese and
    Toasted Walnuts, 11

Halibut, Orange-Cranberry, 122
Hansen, Michelle "Mike," 81, 101

Jack Daniel's Sauce, 116
Jackson Lake Lodge, 143

Kahlua Crème Anglaise, 149
Kaibab Chicken, 25, 35
Key Lime Ice-Box Cheesecake with
    Pistachio Crust, 71

Lake McDonald Lodge, 155–56
Lasagna, Garden Phyllo, 109
Lasagna, Spinach and Mushroom, 74
Lavender-Sweet Corn Custard, 62
Lemon Caper Cream Sauce, 158
Lemon-Thyme Butter, 164
Lime Paste, 93
Lime Sour Cream, 26, 31
Linguica: Sweet Corn Bisque with
    Pumpkin Seeds and, 12
Linguini Vongole, 163
Longmire Sandwich, 121

Mango Salsa, 137, 139
Many Glacier Hotel, 154
Marionberry Crème Brûlé, 101, 107
Marionberry Dressing, 108
Marionberry Syrup, 108
Mather, Stephen P., 55
Mayo, Zesty, 94, 95
Meatloaf, Bison, 162
Meatloaf, Bourbon Buffalo, 116
Miso Vinaigrette, 34
Montana Banana Split, 159
Moose Drool Buffalo Strip Loin, 167
Mount Hood National Forest, 126–31
Mount Rainier National Park, 110–15
Mozzarella, Napoleon of Organic Heirloom
    Tomatoes and, 147
mushrooms
    in Garden Phyllo Lasagna, 109
    in Longmire Sandwich, 121
    Mushroom Sauce, 162, 163
    Scallop and Shitake Mushroom Wellington, 64
    Spinach and Mushroom Lasagna, 74
    Stuffed Portobello Mushrooms, 120
    Wild Mushroom Ragout, 52

Napoleon of Organic Heirloom Tomatoes and
    Buffalo Mozzarella, 147
national parks, 1–2
Navajo Eggplant, 42
New York Strip Steaks with Béarnaise Sauce, 35
Nobile, Joseph, 2, 20–21
nopalitos
    Crispy Cactus Appetizer, 88
    in Rattlesnake Empanadas, 83

Old Faithful Inn, 7–9
Onion Soup, French, 104
Orange-Cranberry Halibut, 122
Orange Pecan Trout, 123
oysters, in Rucko Stuffing, 164

Pancetta Soup, Tuscan, 81, 91
Pan-Roasted Wild Pacific Salmon, 148
Pan-Seared Salmon Tostada, 21, 29
Paradise Inn, 113–15
Pasta Sublime, 25, 32
Pear Vinaigrette, 118, 119
peppers and chiles
    in Avocado Aioli, 72
    in Bison Meatloaf, 162
    in Buffalo Stew, 125
    Chile-Lime Rice, 29, 31
    Chile-Olive Oil, 29, 31
    in Corn and Bean Salsa, 90
    in Corn and Potato Hash, 73
    in Fire-Roasted Corn Salsa, 29, 30
    in Garden Phyllo Lasagna, 109
    in Longmire Sandwich, 121
    in Mango Salsa, 137
    in Rattlesnake Empanadas, 83
    Roasted Tomato-Bell Pepper Sauce, 74, 76
    in Stir-Fried Cabbage, 15
    Sweet Chile Dipping Sauce, 61, 63
    in Western Tenderloin Hash, 86
    in White Turkey Chili, 67
pesto, 158
Pheasant Dumplings, 51
Pickled Quail Eggs, 51
Pico de Gallo, 42, 45
Pie, Boysenberry, 68
Pine Nut Pie, 77
Pistachio Crust, Key Lime Ice-Box
    Cheesecake with, 71
Plum Tomato Confit, 64, 65
Ponzu, 60, 61
Pork Loin, Fruit of the Forest, 124
Pork Tenderloin, Cinnamon-Dusted, 160
Portobello Mushrooms, Stuffed, 120
Port Wine Sauce, 76, 77
Potato Hash, Corn and, 73
prickly pear
    Prickly Pear-Smoked Trout Salad, 44
    Prickly Pear Sticky Buns, 87
    Prickly Pear Vinaigrette, 44
Prince of Wales Hotel, 157
prosciutto, in Charred and Peppered
    Salmon Club, 66

Quail Eggs, Pickled, 51

Rattlesnake Empanadas, 81, 83
Rice, Chile-Lime, 29, 31
Risotto, Roasted Shallot, 147
Roasted Granny Apple Bisque, 58
Roasted Shallot Demi-Glace, 62, 63
Roasted Shallot Risotto, 147

Roasted Tomato-Bell Pepper Sauce, 74, 76
Roasted Vegetable Broth, 57
Rub, Southwestern Spice, 77
Rucko Stuffing, 164

salad
    Grilled Pear Salad, 11
    Prickly Pear-Smoked Trout Salad, 44
    Smoked Salmon Spinach Salad, 34
    Southwest Chicken Salad, 90
    Watermelon, Tomato, and Feta Salad, 135
    Yakima Spinach Salad, 118
salad dressings
    Marionberry Dressing, 108
    Miso Vinaigrette, 34
    Pear and Cranberry Dressing, 118, 119
    Pear Vinaigrette, 118, 119
    Prickly Pear Vinaigrette, 44
    Truffle Vinaigrette, 64, 65
salmon. See fish
salsas and sauces
    Apple-Ginger Compote, 58, 59
    Avocado Aioli, 72
    Béchamel Sauce, 73, 74
    Chile-Olive Oil, 29, 31
    Cholula Hot Sauce, 160, 162
    Corn and Bean Salsa, 90
    Fire-Roasted Corn Salsa, 29, 30
    Gouda Cream Sauce, 105
    Jack Daniel's Sauce, 116
    Lemon Caper Cream Sauce, 158
    Lime Sour Cream, 29, 31
    Mango Salsa, 137, 139
    Marionberry Syrup, 108
    Mushroom Sauce, 162
    pesto, 158
    Pico de Gallo, 45
    Plum Tomato Confit, 64, 65
    Ponzu, 60, 61
    Port Wine Sauce, 76, 77
    Roasted Shallot Demi-Glace, 62, 63
    Roasted Tomato-Bell Pepper Sauce, 74, 76
    Strawberry Sauce, 69
    Sweet Chile Dipping Sauce, 61, 63
    Tomato-Onion Chutney, 144
    Turkish Dill Sauce, 136
    See also dips and spreads; salad dressings
sandwich, Charred and Peppered Salmon Club, 66
Sandwich, Longmire, 121
Santa Fe Steak, 45
sausage, in Sweet Corn Bisque with Linguica and
    Pumpkin Seeds, 12
Scallop and Shitake Mushroom Wellington, 64
seafood
    Clam Chowder, 102
    Crabmeat Gyoza, 61
    Dungeness Crab Sundae, 144
    Linguini Vongole, 163
    Rucko Stuffing, 164
    Scallop and Shitake Mushroom Wellington, 64
    See also fish
Seared Elk Medallions with Madeira Sauce, 9, 15
Shallot Demi-Glace, Roasted, 62, 63

Shallot Risotto, Roasted, 147
Shitake Mushroom Wellington, Scallop and, 64
Shortcake, Strawberry-Poppy Seed, 69
shrimp, in Rucko Stuffing, 164
Sierra Nevada Pale Ale, 56
Sirloin, Char-Grilled, with Caramelized Onions
    and Blue Cheese, 166
Smoked Gouda and Artichoke Dip, 135
Smoked Salmon Spinach Salad, 34
soup
    Black Bean Soup, 26
    Carrot-Ginger Soup, 91
    Chilled Organic Carrot Soup, 139
    Clam Chowder, 102
    Fiscalini Farms Cheddar Cheese Soup, 56
    French Onion Soup, 104
    Roasted Granny Apple Bisque, 58
    Roasted Vegetable Broth, 57
    Sweet Corn Bisque with Linguica and
        Pumpkin Seeds, 12
    Tuscan Pancetta Soup, 81, 91
Sourdough Croutons, 57
Southwest Chicken Salad, 90
Southwestern Spice Rub, 77
Spice Rub, Southwestern, 77
spinach
    in Garden Phyllo Lasagna, 109
    in Kaibab Chicken, 35
    with Navajo Eggplant, 42
    in Scallop and Shitake Mushroom Wellington,
        64
    in Smoked Gouda and Artichoke Dip, 135
    Smoked Salmon Spinach Salad, 34
    Spinach and Mushroom Lasagna, 74
    Spinach Dip, 88
    Yakima Spinach Salad, 118
squash
    in Garden Phyllo Lasagna, 109
    in Longmire Sandwich, 121
    Summer Squash Pancakes, 136
steak
    Char-Grilled Sirloin with Caramelized Onions
        and Blue Cheese, 166
    Grilled Kobe Beef Tri-Tip with Upland Cress,
        62
    New York Strip Steaks with Béarnaise Sauce, 35
    Santa Fe Steak, 45
Stew, Buffalo, 125
Stir-Fried Cabbage, 15
Strawberry-Poppy Seed Shortcake, 69
Strawberry Sauce, 69
Stritzinger, Robert, 55
Stuffed Mojave Chicken, 93
Stuffed Portobello Mushrooms, 120
Stuffing, Rucko, 164
Summer Squash Pancakes, 136
Sweet Chile Dipping Sauce, 61, 63
Sweet Corn Bisque with Linguica and
    Pumpkin Seeds, 12
Syrup, Marionberry, 108

Tamales, Blue Corn, 27
Tenderloin Hash, Western, 86

Timberline Lodge, 129–31
tomatillos, in Navajo Eggplant, 42
tomatoes
    Breaded Wild Alaska Salmon with Heirloom
        Tomato Concassé, 13
    in Fire-Roasted Corn Salsa, 29. 30
    in Kaibab Chicken, 35
    Napoleon of Organic Heirloom Tomatoes and
        Buffalo Mozzarella, 147
    in Pasta Sublime, 25, 32
    Plum Tomato Confit, 64, 65
    in Prickly Pear-Smoked Trout Salad, 44
    Roasted Tomato-Bell Pepper Sauce, 74, 76
    in Southwest Chicken Salad, 90
    Tomato-Onion Chutney, 144
    in Tuscan Pancetta Soup, 91
    Watermelon, Tomato, and Feta Salad, 135
    in Western Tenderloin Hash, 86
trout. See fish
Truffle Vinaigrette, 64, 65
Turkey Chili, White, 55, 67
Turkish Dill Sauce, 136
Tuscan Pancetta Soup, 81, 91

vegetable dishes
    Corn and Potato Hash, 73
    Garden Phyllo Lasagna, 109
    Grilled Artichokes, 105
    Lavender-Sweet Corn Custard, 62
    Navajo Eggplant, 42
    Spinach and Mushroom Lasagna, 74
    Stir-Fried Cabbage, 15
    Stuffed Portobello Mushrooms, 120
    Summer Squash Pancakes, 136
    Wild Mushroom Ragout, 52
    See also beans
vinaigrettes. See salad dressings
Vongole, Linguini, 163

Wallace, James, 143
Walnuts, Candied, 118
Wassail Punch, 72
Watercress, Grilled Kobe Beef Tri-Tip with, 62
Watermelon, Tomato, and Feta Salad, 135
Wawona Hotel, 53–55
Western Tenderloin Hash, 86
Whatley, Percy, 52
Whipped Cream, Grand Marnier with, 69
White Bean-Artichoke Spread, 60
White Turkey Chili, 55, 67
Wild Alaska Salmon Cakes, 94
Wild Mushroom Ragout, 52

Yakima Spinach Salad, 118
Yellowstone National Park, 4–9
Yosemite National Park, 46–55

Zesty Mayo, 94, 95
Zion National Park, 36–41
zucchini. See squash